# Dragonolia

Skyhorse Publishing

Skyhorse Publishing books may be purchased in bulk at special discounts for sales promotion, corporate gifts, fund-raising, or educational purposes. Special editions can also be created to specifications. For details, contact the Special Sales Department, Skyhorse Publishing, 307 West 36th Street, 11th Floor, New York, NY 10018 or info@skyhorsepublishing.com.

Skyhorse® and Skyhorse Publishing® are registered trademarks of Skyhorse Publishing, Inc.®, a Delaware corporation. Visit our website at www.skyhorsepublishing.com.

Visit our website at www.skyhorsepublishing.com.

10 9 8 7 6 5 4 3 2 1

Library of Congress Cataloging-in-Publication Data is available on file.

Cover design by Brian Peterson

ISBN: 978-1-634-50327-3

Ebook ISBN: 978-1-510-70092-5

Printed in China

# Dragonolia

## 14 Tales and Craft Projects for the Creative Adventurer

CHRIS BARNARDO

*with a foreword*
*by*
*Sir Richard Barons*

Sir Richard Barons outside Barons' Dragonolia shop in about 1900, after an inspection to make sure that the shop was ready to be opened to customers for the first time. The shop was successful but the last of its kind, and closed down in 1925.

# Contents

*This volume is dedicated to
the wonderful crew who
made these voyages possible:
Dawn, India, James, William, and Alexander.
May we have many more
exciting adventures together.*

Dear Reader,

*Dragonolia* is a storybook with a difference. Read on and you will discover fourteen charming tales, each one intertwined with a wonderful craft project that will make it possible for you, the reader (or the listener, if this story is being read to you), to relive my adventures as a dragon hunter, in the safety and comfort of your own home. There is no doubt that you will find the tales thoroughly enjoyable at any time, but they are singularly appropriate for reading aloud at bedtime, when they will not only prepare one for restful slumber, but also create a happy expectation of the wonderful project that will undoubtedly be tackled the following morning.

These short stories have been compiled from the many notes, sketches, and diaries I have collected over the years and detail my now famous expeditions to bring back numerous weird and wonderful artifacts from the most unlikely of places. This is my first collection of short stories, and from it I hope you will get an interesting glimpse into the life of the gentleman-adventurer and the many quirky mishaps that befall such a chap. My enduring motto, *Life Is Your Adventure*, is as true now as it ever was; so buckle up and make it yours! It's still the perfect call-to-action for explorers of every age.

I sincerely hope that you will enjoy hearing about my exploits, and also re-creating some of my favorite artifacts, so that you might begin to build your own private collection of beautiful dragonolia relics.

All that remains for me to do is wish you good luck on your journey through this little window on to my treasured past, and every success in making the projects contained herein. Additional material and downloads can be found at www.dragonolia.com.

Your humble servant,

*Sir Richard Barons*

Sir Richard Barons

LOCAL DRAGON TRACKER, CHARMER & SIR RICHARD BARONS 1922

Sir Richard Barons (right) with a local dragon tracker and charmer, in Ngari, the highest point on the Qinghai-Tibetan Plateau, in 1922, on a trek to discover (for conservationist purposes) the last example of a wild Chinese lung, living in Tibet.

If ye should thieve

The dragon roe,

Tread quiet and slight

When in her glow.

Though stopp'd in

Restful sleep she seems,

Ne'er wake her

From her golden dreams,

For with deadly eye

And hardened scale,

Her tooth shall be

Your coffin nail.

# Shadow Box Frame

## The tale of the lost mink that was the cause of an invention

I can't be sure, but I am reasonably certain that my family were the inventors of the shadow box. I say my family, however that is not technically correct, the credit should more properly go to my father's housekeeper.

As a child, my father was not at all well-mannered. Of course, he grew up to become the world renowned Lord Barons, but those who knew him well knew also that even with his advancing years and

increasing respectability, a small corner of his soul forever ran with the mischievous streak that as a child had resulted in more canings than he cared to remember. One particular escapade I never tired of hearing about was the tale of the lost mink. Over the years the story seems to have been embellished with numerous extravagant exaggerations; nevertheless even today, the core truth of the tale can be verified by a quick jaunt down to the East Wing corridor. There, hung on the wall are fifteen or sixteen (I forget exactly how many) ancient shadow box frames. The contents of some are remarkable (the collection of dragon scales has never been equaled), but for the most part, what lurks within them is not half as interesting as the tale of what lies behind each box.

In July 1825, my father was home from school for the summer holiday and within one week had become bored and determined to catch and train a wild mink, with the intention of putting on a miniature circus show for one or other of the famous guests that were staying at the house over the summer months. Insofar as a plan might have been said to be panning out, a mink had indeed been trapped and although completely wild, had been kept in captivity for at least a week in a makeshift cage the groundsman had hastily thrown together. Even my father's considerable diligence in the endeavour of the beast's domestication had had absolutely no effect on calming its feral nature, and two weeks into the training program, the only trick it seemed to have mastered was that of delivering

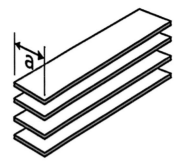

**STEP 1.** Cut four strips of thick cardboard. Make sure that they are exactly the same width as each other and the edges are parallel. Use a ruler to make sure they are the same width as each other.

**STEP 2.** Get an off-cut (tester sample) of some embossed wallpaper, and using either spray glue or white glue, wrap each cardboard strip in the paper as neatly as possible. Don't worry too much about the back, no one is going to be looking there.

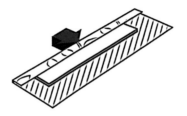

**STEP 3.** To make your miter guide, accurately trace the diagonal on the template sheet and cut out. This can be done with scissors, but you'll probably get a better result using a craft knife and ruler.

**STEP 4.** Fold the miter guide horizontally, making sure you fold it accurately. Place it on the back of the wrapped strip and mark off the miter. Mark off both ends so that you make a trapezium shape—i.e., longer along one edge than the other.

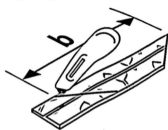

**STEP 5.** Using a ruler and craft knife, carefully cut along each miter. Make sure to hold the knife upright so that your cut is vertical. It is also **VERY IMPORTANT** to make sure that you cut your strip lengths in matching pairs so that dimension b is the same, otherwise you will not be able to make right angle corners on your frame.

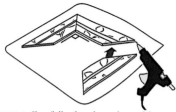

**STEP 6.** Carefully glue the edges of the frame together. You can use white glue for this, but it is much quicker to use a glue gun. Lay the frame flat, and to make sure that it doesn't stick to the table, lay it on a piece of cling film. Take care that each piece is stuck at right angles to the other pieces; otherwise your frame will have gaps at the corners.

a vicious bite to anyone witless enough to put their fingers within a muzzle's reach of the cage bars. Consequently, feeding it could only be attempted while wearing the toughest dragonhide gloves. However, despite the lack of civilizing progress, my father doted on the animal and maintained that he would eventually tame it.

It was during the third week that calamity struck. My father had taken to leaving the cage in the East Wing corridor. He claimed it was cooler there and in any case, he planned to make that the venue of his mini-circus, and felt that it might be as well to acclimatize the creature to its new environment as part of his instructive regime. One morning, after breakfast, my father visited the cage and found the creature to be lying lifeless in one of its corners. No amount of coaxing, even with pieces of the best fillet steak, were able to elicit so much as a halfhearted nibble, let alone the ferocious bite of which the brute was known to be capable of delivering. Fearing the worst and throwing caution to the wind, my father opened the cage fully and gently lifted the mink clear. Once free of the cage, the creature made a miraculous recovery and leapt from my father's arms, making off at a lightning sprint down the hallway. About halfway down the hall there was a hole in the wainscot boarding and the mink wasted no time in disappearing into it and thence into the wall cavity. Initially my father was beside himself, but within minutes had collected his wits enough to have retrieved a hammer from the stable block and was busy running up and down the corridor knocking holes in the lath and plaster wall in an attempt to find the animal and return it to the "comfort" of its cage.

He had made about five such holes of varying sizes when his activity was brought to an abrupt halt by the bellowing voice of my grandfather, who having been alerted to the commotion by the housekeeper had wasted no time in apprising himself of the situation at first hand.

"Stand clear, boy," he boomed, raising his trusty twelve bore to his good eye. "I'll get the blighter."

My father knew better than to argue. My grandfather was not known to stop for anyone, and even at fifty years of age was thought still to

**STEP 7.** For an antique wood effect, paint the frame with an undercoat of brown. Of course depending on what type of embossed paper you used and what look you are aiming for, you can paint it any color you want.

**STEP 8.** To get the antique effect, spray only the edges in a darker color or black. Lightly spray the black just enough to give a slightly darker edge, to make the frame look as though it is very old.

**STEP 9.** Pick out the embossing in a contrasting color. For the old antique wood effect, use gold rubbing paste and gently rub it over the embossed paper so that it catches only the raised parts. For other colors, try washing on and wiping off different colors to get a great distressed effect. Alternatively paint the raised part of the design to pick out the detail. This leaf pattern, for example, could be painted in lovely rich greens and browns to look just like real leaves.

**STEP 10.** Paint the back of the frame black. This hides most things. However, if you have made a pale colored frame, then you might want to paint the back in a cream color or white.

**STEP 11.** Place the frame upside down on to some thick mounting board and mark off the size of the frame window.

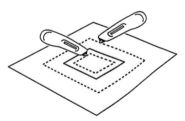

**STEP 12.** Mark around inside the drawn line by as much as the width of the mounting boarder of inner frame you want showing in the box frame window. Also mark around the outside of the line by about 2 inches (5 cm). Neatly cut out the center and round the edge to make your mounting border.

have had the keenest eye in all of Hertfordshire. Without protest my father ducked down and ran to the back of the hall, hoping against hope that the mink might still somehow escape.

By this time most of the household, including one or two of the houseguests, had assembled at one end of the hall, and were agog with anticipation. My grandfather bade the audience silent. A faint scratching was heard, followed almost immediately by the most deafening report as my grandfather discharged his shotgun into the wall exactly where he believed the varmint to be. Needless to say he missed with the first shot, although he did succeed in dislodging a fair amount of plaster and a huge quantity of dust. It took a further nine or ten thunderous blasts to dispatch the mink. A miniature circus it was not, but a spectacle worthy of the local press it most definitely was, and it remained the talk of many a lively bar evening for years to come.

Quite unexpectedly my father did not get the accustomed caning for his misdemeanours over the lost mink that he expected. It was said that my grandfather just lightly cuffed him around the ear and grinning like a Cheshire Cat, took him down to the library, and although he was only thirteen years old, poured him his first whiskey.

It fell to the housekeeper to get the damage repaired, but this was the summer of 1825, and there was a dearth of plasterers. So as to quickly cover the holes she was obligated to design, and have made, a set of deep, glass-lidded box frames and have arranged within each a little cameo of artifacts. The largest box was saved for the hapless mink, which was duly stuffed and mounted therein and hung in pride of place at the end of the hall.

As the story spread beyond the immediate locality, it was not long before anyone who was anyone judged their status in the more fashionable circles by whether or not they had stood in the now infamous East Wing and looked the ill-fated mink, eye to (glass) eye, presented as it now was, in its charming box frame. Within a year, similar box frames were adorning the more contemporary Victorian walls up and down the country and had gained the name of "shadow boxes," on account of the strange shadows their sides cast over the contents of the box.

**STEP 13.** Cut a thin sheet of clear plastic the same size as the mounting boarder and glue to the back of the frame. Use any thin piece of clear plastic packing or an OHP slide. Once the glue has set, glue the mounting border to the frame over the clear plastic film. TIP: it helps to get things straight if you turn over the frame and look through the window as you are sticking it to the mounting border.

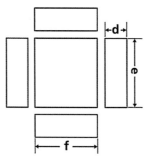

**STEP 14.** To make the display box cut a rectangle of card the same size as the mounting border (e x f). Now cut two rectangles d wide and e long and two rectangles d wide and f long, where d is the depth of the box you want.

**STEP 15.** Paint the box black, inside and out. Once again, if you have chosen to make a light colored box then you might want to paint the box a light color.

**STEP 16.** Mount your object or artifact in the box. If you need a name plaque, design one and stick this under the object.

**STEP 17.** Put four small spots of glue on the top edge of the box and glue the frame over it so that the object appears centrally in the window. Use only a dab of glue so that you can open the box if you want to change the contents later.

**STEP 18.** Trace the leg from the template page, cut out, and stick it to a piece of cardboard. Cut it out and paint it to match the color of your box. Rest the frame on a flat surface, and tilting it back at a slight angle, glue the single leg centrally on the back so that it also rests on the flat surface.

I have heard that some über-modish souls even went as far as to "prepare" the walls with a suitable firearm prior to hanging their shadow box, but I cannot say for certain if such a thing ever really happened.

Since then, shadow boxes have become world famous and are a great way to display precious memorabilia. Now you can easily make one. This box frame displays my precious set of dragon scales. Later I will explain in detail how to make those, but for now, if you would like to join the ranks of the fashionable, all you have to do is follow my simple instructions. I'm sure you will make an excellent job of it.

**Tracing templates**

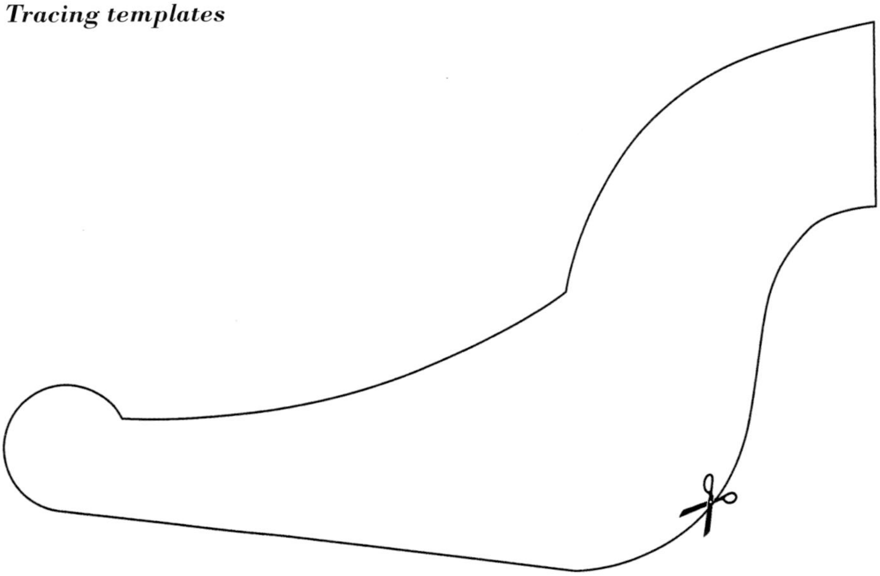

## *a.*

*leg outline*

*Trace on to thick card, cut out card, and stick leg to back of box if you want a table mounted box frame.*

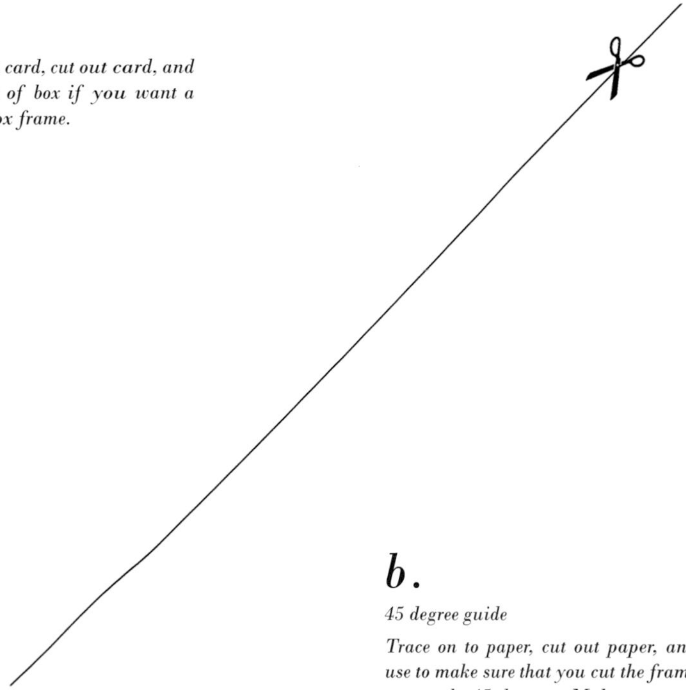

## *b.*

*45 degree guide*

*Trace on to paper, cut out paper, and use to make sure that you cut the frame at exactly 45 degrees. Make sure you trace and cut out accurately.*

# Antique Chart

## Dream of an undiscovered country and the art of mapmaking

**W**hile working late in the map room doing some research for my next campaign, I chanced to come across an old chart that I had not seen before. I would have dismissed it immediately if I had not recognised my father's flowing handwritten notes. Accompanying the map were a few journal pages, amongst which was this intriguing passage.

\* \* \*

'Tis curious the tricks that may be played upon the mind by a creaking ship, a lack of sleep, and an absence of sufficient sustenance; but I am certain that the lights I saw that night were no illusion.

I naturally require little sleep. While traveling by boat, even the gentle rhythmic roll of the deep sea swell and the velvet inky blackness of the vast oceanic night never afford me any more than three or four hours of restless dozing. It is mostly for this reason that I always agree to take the middle watch, which I find not only alleviates the boredom, but usually endears me to the crew, who to a man, would rather be tucked up snugly in their bunks at the witching hour. Although we had been forced to take this trip late in the year, the night was warm and until then had been uneventful, given as it was to a calm sea and a soft steady wind of about five knots, driving us steadily southeast. Nevertheless, we remained in the grip of a powerful current that by the quartermaster's reckoning had put us at least two degrees off our intended course and we were in uncharted waters. We had been at

**STEP 1.** Print out the blank map template from www.dragonolia.com. Carefully cut it out to remove the white edge if you want.

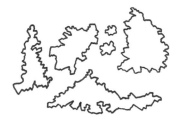

**STEP 2.** Design and draw your islands or country. Use a wiggly line and make lots of little islands near the main one. Remember to draw coves, bays, and river inlets.

**STEP 3.** Draw in the rivers and sea routes linking some of the smaller islands with the main one. Use a dashed line for the sea routes.

sea for many weeks and were running short of provisions and our boat, sturdy as she was, was in urgent need of repair.

The moonless night was as dark as pitch and there was nothing to see across the vast expanse of glossy black water that stretched in every direction, save the occasional starlight glint reflected from the Milky Way, stretching from horizon to horizon like a vast sparkling bow, an unfathomable distance above our heads. I knew of no land within two weeks' sailing of our current location, so you will understand my misgivings when suddenly I caught sight of what appeared to be an island, dead ahead. As we drew nearer to the land, it became clear that this was no fist of barren rock pushing its way up from the depths of the abyss, but a lush and inhabited island beckoning us forth with twinkling lights and all the allure of Plymouth Quay on Midsummer's Eve. I did not dismiss my caution, however, as I knew not whether the people of this unexpected land would be civilized or barbarous and cruel. As we approached within hailing distance of the island, I considered the possibility that the locals might welcome us to dinner as an unexpected entrée, rather than as their guests. I knew this to be a fate that had befallen other hapless mariners unlucky enough to run into the wrong sort of native. Believing discretion to be the better part of valor, I decided that until we had established the inhabitants' temperament, it would be prudent for us to proceed with stealth. Treading lightly, I made my way to the vessel's stern and woke the Master, whom I ordered to extinguish all lamps and maintain a quiet ship. When the shore was but one league distant we hove to and I had the First Mate take me ashore in the skiff.

With my heart pounding in my chest, we beached the dinghy in silence and gingerly made our way up the foreshore toward the lights we had seen from the boat. My fear of a tragic reception began to ebb away when we came upon a row of simple fishing smacks, all smartly stowed, with brilliant white sails tightly furled, almost glowing in the starlight. In fact, my fear was soon replaced by curiosity as we neared the outskirts of the village and I heard the sound of laughter and music coming from a sturdy looking but brightly lit building that was doing a very good job of looking every bit like the local tavern. From the few small snatches of conversation I caught as we approached, I decided that the language, which I had never heard before, was a strange mixture of French and English. However, as I speak French with reasonable fluency, I felt certain that I would be able to make myself understood.

Once inside the tavern, I quickly established that the townsfolk were indeed friendly and within the hour the entire ship's company had landed and were making merry in the bright little hostelry, on what we now knew to be called Dragon Island.

Over the weeks that followed we were given every assistance in repairing our vessel and stocking it for our continued journey. In return we employed our best cartographers to prepare charts of the whole archipelago—something that the locals sorely needed. The task took many weeks and when it was complete, we had all grown so accustomed to

**STEP 4.** Around the edge of each piece of land draw short straight horizontal lines; also fill in any lakes with the same horizontal lines.

**STEP 5.** Mark in your main cities and towns. Either draw shapes for the cities or little pictures of groups of houses, add the odd spire or castle. Join the towns with roads. Name your towns, roads, and rivers. Be creative when naming them.

**STEP 6.** Name your islands and the seas with names written neatly in capitals using the letter guide in this chapter, or use flowing copperplate script. For the best effect space out your letters to cover the area the name refers to, just like a real map.

the locals and their easy, simple way of living, that we barely felt able to leave their wonderful haven. It was with heavy hearts that we bade our farewells and set sail, but as we did, we stowed copies of the charts and vowed to return the following year.

A year passed, and then another and I am ashamed to say that a full decade had elapsed before I was able to mount a return expedition. We sailed directly to the recorded position of the island, but despite our best efforts we could not locate even a single scrap of land.

It is now more than forty years since that strange enchanted escapade and today, even after three further attempts to find that mysterious isle, all that remains as proof of our landfall and the many happy weeks spent there are faded copies of the maps that we prepared for the locals during our stay. Even now as I gaze upon these faint lines, I wonder if in fact those lights I spied that night while taking the middle watch had been just an illusion after all. Nevertheless, I leave this map to assist any adventurers that might desire to follow me in their efforts to find Dragon Island.

\* \* \*

I sat back in my chair, my curiosity piqued by such a fanciful story. My father had never told me this tale. He was not given to exaggeration and had been one of the most respected and experienced adventurers of the age, so the account certainly had merit. I was definitely intrigued, but after some deliberation, I resolved to put the map back in the drawer and not trouble myself to look for an island my father had failed to find after numerous attempts to do so. Strange things can happen to the mind in the Southern Seas on a long voyage, and it is quite possible that the whole affair was a figment of some sort of collective derangement.

As for the map, though, it has inspired me, and I wonder if you would enjoy the process of designing a map of an island of your own whimsical invention. I have had our London cartographer prepare a blank map template, which you may print off, from our special download facility at www. dragonolia.com. I have also prepared some special instructions on the map creation technique, which are provided here for your reference and enjoyment.

**STEP 7.** Color around the edge of each piece of land with blue pencil.

**STEP 8.** Color inside each piece of land with green pencil. Color in small islands completely.

**STEP 9.** Draw some monsters in the sea and on the land. Draw in caves, mountains, and any other features that you think will be of interest to travelers visiting the island you discovered and charted.

# Filigree Egg Case

## The inspiration for the most famous of jewelry eggs

One of my earliest memories is of looking up at a wonderfully detailed painting of the golden filigree egg case that was hung on my nursery wall. The egg case looked so real that I felt I might easily have been able to reach up, pluck it out of the picture, and hold its radiant, glowing form in my little fist, like an ember snatched from the blackened stones of the fancifully depicted dragon's nest by which it lay.

As soon as I could read, and was permitted entry to our library, scarcely an evening would go by that wouldn't find me sitting in my favorite reading chair with an enormous leather-bound copy of St. John Chrysostom's *Nature's Beasts* crushing my knees, hungrily scouring the text for the tiniest fact about the golden egg case and the fire-breathing beast that was commonly credited with its creation. Occasionally I would come across other drawings of the glittering eggs-haped lattice, and I would study them for hours hoping to unlock the fabled object's strange mystical tangle. Of course, in those days, its actual existence was in question, despite the fact that over the years many adventurers returning from the Himalayas had claimed to have seen it on their travels. Occasionally stories of such sightings surfaced in the press, but no gallery or museum could boast a single fragment of its golden filigree, let alone a complete and undamaged example.

As I grew up the thought of being the first person to successfully find and bring back such a fabulous prize haunted me. When I was old enough to try my hand at the task, yet still young enough not to dismiss the folly of such an exercise, I put all my energy and a substantial fraction of our family fortune into mounting an expedition to recover the golden filigree egg case for the Barons' private collection.

We set off in the spring of 1872 and after a tolerable sea voyage and a lengthy but uneventful overland trek, we arrived in Kathmandu still keen for the challenge. After a couple of weeks' rest, the final leg of our journey took us directly to our camp

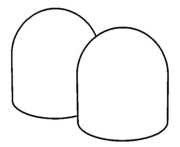

**STEP 1.** Take two identical round-ended personal care product tops—deodorant or shaving foam, for example.

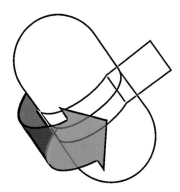

**STEP 2.** Neatly tape them together to make an egg shape.

**STEP 3.** Drill a small hole at the center of one end and glue-gun glue a cocktail stick through the hole to act as a handle for the next steps.

just outside Gorak Shep, the highest village in Nepal and as near as we dare set up to the most recent recorded sightings of the Golden Lung, creator and guardian of the only known example of the golden filigree egg case.

On the first evening the Sherpas joined us in the main tent for a nightcap of the most evil tasting wood spirit, the drinking of which, we had discovered, was the only way to keep warm through the freezing Nepalese nights. When our stomachs were full and the general hubbub of voices had quietened, our head guide began to relate his family's tales of the ancient fire-breather and her various strange and glorious ways. His eyes sparkled like evening rubies in the warm glow of the camp firelight as he told us the stories that his great-grandfather had told him many years before.

As everyone knows, over its incredibly long life, the mighty Golden Lung has gathered and now jealously guards a priceless treasure hoard. However, despite its huge size and immense power, the dragon herself is an anxious creature and during the centuries has developed the neurotic habit of gnawing at such pieces of gold that she might conveniently grasp in her terrible claws. Pure gold is soft and the dragon's

teeth are by many degrees harder, and inevitably the dragon swallows some of the gold. The noble metal may not stay in the dragon's body for long, but by some infernal mechanism is laid out as a network of fine golden filaments over the surface of her eggs before they are laid. The villagers thereabouts had long believed that this "golden filigree" had actually served a purpose beneficial to the unhatched dragon chicks, as the thick metallic veins crisscrossing the eggs appeared to protect the otherwise surprisingly delicate eggshells from cracking as they rolled over the sharp flinty stones that littered the dragon's nest.

The shadows wobbled with the guttering of the candles as the gravelly voice of the old man brought forth tale after tale of the dragon. A dragon that for all we knew might well have been flying high in the sky over our heads, at that very moment, dark and silent in the cold night air.

The next morning we set off early, before it was properly light. My plan was simple: to search for and discover the lair of the brooding Golden Lung, before she returned from her nightly hunt, so that we might approach the nest when she was absent and scour the surrounding parts for discarded egg cases, while avoiding detection by the Draco Beast herself.

The dragon's lair was not difficult to locate. Her blackened, smoldering nest looked more like a used-up hearth than a place of comfort and stood out like a cattle brand, seared on to the pale rump of the icy scree. However, we did have considerable trouble finding a discarded egg case. Even with the dragon away hunting, we dared not get too close to the nest, in case she came back and decided that we made a pre-luncheon appetizer. Day after day we made the arduous trip from the camp to the nest and back, gulping the thin icy mountain air like drowning fish, treading without noise so as not to be discovered by the fire-breathing beast. Although we never actually saw the dragon, we lived in constant fear of being discovered and knew that as the days went by, the chances of our detection increased greatly as we looked longer and longer and drew closer and closer to the nest itself. After a month of this tiring work the whole party was becoming disheartened. At the six-week mark, one of our number became seriously ill, and it was with a heavy heart that I was forced to admit failure and pack up camp. On the day

# Filigree Egg Case

**STEP 4.** Lightly coat the whole of the surface of the egg shape in vegetable oil or silicone furniture (or shoe) polish.

**STEP 5.** Holding the cocktail stick handle rotate the egg and cover it in thin streams of glue-gun glue to make a filigree matrix over the surface.

**STEP 6.** Using a sharp craft knife carefully cut through the glue-gun glue (when it has set) from top to bottom on only one side of the egg.

of our departure, I made one last trip back to the nest in a final desperate attempt to find an egg case. It was the afternoon when I reached the nest and from five hundred yards away I could see the dragon had returned. Not to be deterred, I inched my way toward the nest. As I got closer the heat radiating off her glistening scales prickled the skin on my face and backs of my hands. Shimmering air rose up from her heaving side, distorting and wobbling the view of the mountain peak behind. She lay sleeping, draped casually over half the nest, crushing it under her enormous weight like a large demolished building that had just toppled over in a cascade of bricks and lay heavily exactly where it had fallen. Her breath came in large bellowing rasps, and with each deeply noisy snore she snorted out huge noxious plumes of foul-smelling gas. Without a thought for my safety I approached to within a few feet of the nest edge, my face stinging in the heat. I could hardly believe it—there, shining under a tuft of scorched fire grass, was the most perfect example of a golden filigree egg case I could have ever dreamt of. Gingerly I took the egg case as I had always dreamt I would and slipped quietly back from the edge of the nest. Dragons are light sleepers so I made as little noise as possible, until I was at least a mile or two distant from her slumbering form.

On the sea passage back to England, I had the pleasure of dining at the Captain's table where I was fortunate to make the acquaintance of the Russian jeweler, Karl Gustavovich Fabergé. He had pressed me to reveal the nature of my trip, and although I am a modest man, it was not long before he had persuaded me to have the ship's safe opened so that I could show him the golden filigree egg case. He took an extraordinary interest in it, an interest whose reason only became clear some ten years later when I heard that he had created an egg-shaped gift for Tzar Alexander III.

The wonderful golden filigree egg case is still in the Barons' private museum, but in the event that your schedule will not permit you to come and see it, you'll be pleased to see that I have provided adequate step-by-step instructions by which method you might make a replica for your own collection.

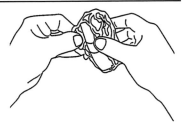

**STEP 7.** Carefully peel the glue-gun glue off the bottle cap egg shape. Glue-gun glue is fairly tough and strong and you may need to work your fingers under the bead to remove it completely.

**STEP 8.** Carefully repair the split in the filigree egg case with a drop of glue-gun glue on each of the filigree elements that you cut through.

**STEP 9.** Holding the egg case on the cocktail stick or other suitable wire, paint or spray it using metallic gold, silver, or copper effect paint.

# Dragonhide Pouch

## Tough negotiations for the toughest hide

s well as the many campaigns I have conducted to bring back exotic and often dangerous exhibits, I have of course had to make my fair share of mundane trips as a matter of routine. One such expedition was to locate and secure a reliable supply of tanned and prepared dragonhide for an old friend of mine who wished to merchandise dragonhide products in a small shop in Bond Street, London. Throughout the industrial revolution, dragonhide was thought to be one of the strongest naturally occurring materials, apparently resistant to all forms of physical and chemical attack. Obviously capable of withstanding great heat and surprisingly able to maintain its flexibility even in extreme cold, the lightweight, breathable, supple-but-tough dragonhide had long been favoured by archers and bowmen for the manufacture of arrow-proof jackets in centuries past. It was these exact properties that led my enterprising friend to consider using the hide for the fabrication of a new type of purse, wallet, or pouch that would be strong enough to be resistant against theft and protect even the most delicate valuables. He had acquired a lease on a smart boutique at the more fashionable end of Bond Street, and had very much fallen in love with the idea of selling these exclusive products to the West End's more affluent shoppers.

In actual fact, although dragonhide is a remarkable material, its surface hardness is only comparable to that of quartz, placing it at about seven on the Mohs hardness scale, and rendering it workable with specialist tools tipped with topaz, corundum, or diamond (where available). In the late nineteenth century, companies capable of tanning dragonhide existed in a few countries, but if one desired the most exquisite workmanship, material of the highest quality, and security of supply, then only the tanneries in Mongolia's capital, Ikh Khuree (as it was known then), would suffice.

While my friend set up his shop, I volunteered to travel to the top of the world in search of the best tanned

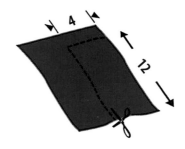

**STEP 1.** Cut out a rectangle of velour, felt or velvet fabric about 12" x 4".

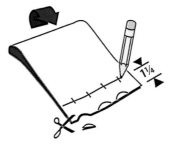

**STEP 2.** Fold the fabric over face side in and cut about four small scallops out of the cut edge. Mark a line across the fabric to get the hole positions neatly aligned.

**STEP 3.** Fold the fabric over at the marked line and cut out four small holes by cutting semicircles through the fold; repeat that the other end.

**STEP 4.** Place face up and put a thin stripe of glue-gun glue as close to the edge as you can, halfway down both sides (as shown).

**STEP 5.** Fold the fabric over, making certain to keep it square and flattened out. Wait for two minutes until the glue has cooled and set.

**STEP 6.** Turn the bag right side out and then carefully dribble glue-gun glue stripes diagonally across the fabric surface. Crisscross them to give a diamond pattern. Do both sides the same.

dragonhide available. The journey, which had been made bearable by the advent of the newly laid railroad, was nevertheless long and arduous. However I found it uneventful enough and the long days in my cabin afforded me ample time to read and write, a luxury that I rarely enjoyed in those busy days.

Needless to say I arrived refreshed and more than ready for the lengthy negotiations with the Shaman Hidemasters in the beautiful capital of Ikh Khüree on the banks of the River Tuul, in the shadow of the Sacred Mountains. From research I had conducted before I set out, I had learned that business discussions with a Mongolian tannery could not be rushed and would only follow after the traditional introductions and appropriate welcoming ceremonies had been conducted according to their custom, and in some cases this could take days as one worked up through the ranks of officials in reverse order of seniority. So you will understand that I was shocked when, on my first day, I was greeted by the Chief Hidemaster himself, actually out in the street, on the steps of the tannery. I fumbled with my traditional token offering of gold and paper but it was brushed aside, and I was quickly ushered in to the dark building. What I learned there shocked me. After nearly two hundred years of preparing and working dragonhide, the Khruee Tannery was to close its doors to business, along with all the other tanneries in Mongolia. New legislation had banned the trade of dragonhide in order to protect the dwindling numbers of dragons, which were being hunted to extinction. In hushed tones I was told that it was only due to my reputation for honor and discretion that was I being offered what was to be their last shipment of dragonhide. Given the desperation in their eyes, I felt that I'd better not try to negotiate too hard with the poor fellows. I drank all the salted yak butter tea I could stomach and our business was conducted within the hour. In the end, I paid considerably more than I had expected for the hides, but felt sure that my friend back in London would thank me richly for acquiring such a prize, especially given that the Mongolian tannery was about to close.

**STEP 7.** When the glue has set, either paint gold on to the glue strips or use Goldfinger or Rub 'n Buff brand antique finger polish to highlight the glue stripes. You can use silver, any metallic paint, or even black if you don't have gold.

**STEP 8.** Thread cord or elastic braid through the holes, in for the first hole and then out and in till you have gone all around the neck of the bag. Tie off the cord in a simple knot.

**STEP 9.** Using another piece of the same cord thread through in the same fashion but starting from the other side. Now when you pull the two knotted ends apart, the bag should close tightly. If it doesn't stay closed, you may have to thread the cords back on themselves one more time.

# Dragonhide Pouch

I returned to England, taking great care that the delivery of the precious cargo proceded without hitch. My friend was thrilled and before six weeks had passed he had built a thriving business selling dragonhide accessories of every kind.

And that might have been the end of the tale had not I chanced to overhear a conversation in my club one afternoon a month or two later. It is not my practice to eavesdrop, you understand, but on this occasion I could not help but take notice of the loud conversation and raucous laughter of a small party sitting at the table next to mine. I pricked up my ears when I heard mention of Mongolian Dragonhide Tanneries and then to my dismay, further laughter at one chap's story of their disreputable practice of selling off old dragonhide to the unknowing traveler, under the pretence that the material was the last of its kind available. I considered approaching their table, but thought better of it when the gentleman in question went on to say that he had heard of "one poor blighter" who had been tricked into buying nearly three hundred pounds worth of last season's dragonhide at nearly twice its market value, after he had been hoodwinked into believing that a ban on the sale of dragonhide was imminent.

I turned my back to them and prayed that no one had recognized me. Later I learned that not only were the Mongolians superior hidemasters, but they were also skilled at the art of *negotiation by deception* and that the scoundrels regularly fabricated tales of restricted supply in order to extract the highest possible prices from unwitting purchasers.

Apparently dragonhide is still widely available and these days a wide variety of equipment exists that permits you to make accessories of your very own.

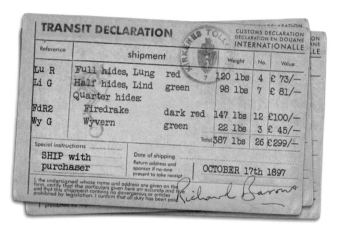

| TRANSIT DECLARATION | | | CUSTOMS DECLARATION DECLARATION EN DOUANE INTERNATIONALLE | | |
|---|---|---|---|---|---|
| Reference | shipment | | Weight | No. | Value |
| Lu R | Full hides, Lung | red | 120 lbs | 4 | £ 73/– |
| Li G | Half hides, Lind | green | 98 lbs | 7 | £ 81/– |
| | Quarter hides: | | | | |
| FdR2 | Firedrake | dark red | 147 lbs | 12 | £100/– |
| Wy G | Wyvern | green | 22 lbs | 3 | £ 45/– |
| | | Total | 387 lbs | 26 | £299/– |

| Special instructions | Date of shipping | |
|---|---|---|
| SHIP with purchaser | Return address and sponsor if no-one present to take receipt | OCTOBER 17th 1897 |

I, the undersigned whose name and address are given on the form, certify that the particulars given here are accurate and true and that this shipment contains no danergerous or articles prohibited by legislation. I confirm that all duty has been paid.

*Richard Barons*

Full transit declaration documents are needed if the hides are to be allowed through customs. Each dragonry is only permitted to import six hundred pounds of hides per year. In practice, a shipment of this size and quality would be sufficient for at least nine months of production.

# Hunters' Goggles

### And other fabulous dragon hunters' apparel

It is true that much has been written about the dangers of dragon hunting. At the height of the dragon hunting boom, toward the end of the nineteenth century, hardly a week went by without the London press running a story of some hapless adventurer who, chancing his luck on a hunt, had either been fried to a crisp in the blast of a superheated roar, or eviscerated on the razor sharp claw of an angry firebelly beast. Still, the lure of the wealth and kudos that could be acquired by hunting, capturing, or even (sadly) slaying a dragon, was a temptation that drove many to take dangerous risks with their own safety. As a result, a whole industry grew up selling specialized protective dragon hunting clothing and equipment. Of course as you might also guess, most of it was peddled by opportunistic merchants keen to make a quick profit out of any adventurer who didn't know better, and was of very little use in the field while actually hunting dragons. You may not know, but I can assure you of the fact that back in Victorian times there were few, if any, man-made materials capable of withstanding the best a fully grown, bad tempered wyvern could deliver when it wanted to.

As with everything, bravery (and some would say reckless, misplaced bravery) has never been a substitute for skill and experience. Despite my numerous forays into dragon country, I never for a moment considered using even the best body armor of the day. Oh yes, as you might imagine I had tried just about every piece of protective garb available. However, generally I used my cunning and skill to stay one step ahead of the dragons I pursued, rather than dress up in silly looking and often restrictive clothing, and the Gorgon's Flame and Heat Proof Hunting Jacket that I was given one Christmas by a slightly dotty aunt stayed over the back of my chair in my study. Even the Amazing Armadillo Claw-Resistant Head Protector, which I received as gift from the King of Prussia, lay unused, in its original box, in my storeroom, for more than ten years. Yet during that time, I never received so much as a scratch

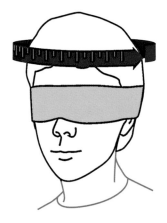

**STEP 1.** Measure around the head. You'll be surprised how big the measurement is. Wrap the thick fabric or leather strip around the head and mark off the length with a permanent marker. Remember to leave some overlap for the Velcro (hook and loop) fixing.

**STEP 2.** Cut out the shape of the goggles using a tracing of the template page as a guide. Cut out the shape, including the eyeholes, using a strong pair of scissors.

**STEP 3.** Cut most of the center from two plastic milk bottle lids so that you leave a small rim round the edge. Take care with sharp knives and only cut soft polythene plastic lids.

**STEP 4.** Paint both closures with gold paint. You can use spray paint, gold felt-tipped markers, or gold paint.

**STEP 5.** Using a tracing of the circle guides on the template page, mark two circles on the top shoulder of a 2 liter PET soda bottle with permanent marker.

**STEP 6.** Cut the top off the soda bottle.

or singed eyebrow from the mighty beasts I hunted.

However, there was one piece of protective apparel that I would never be without—my Flare Resistant Glaremaster Goggles; but then of course, these are no ordinary ocular protection. They had the sort of exotic technology in them that might only have been dreamt of these days; extremely lightweight, finely-ground sapphire lenses were able to automatically adjust how dark they were via the employment of a small electric current and secret, patented machinery, so that the wearer's normal vision might be maintained regardless of the viewing conditions. Blinding flash flares from the nostrils of an angered dragon were instantaneously dimmed, yet by some infernal mechanism dark caves needed no illumination, as the Glaremaster Goggles boosted any available light, however feeble, in order to enhance one's vision, without any adjustment by the wearer, so as to render the carriage of lamps unnecessary. As dragons like hiding in the darkest corners of the darkest caves so that they might pounce from the shadows on the unlucky hunter, this feature alone saved my life on numerous occasions as I crept up on dragons who thought they were all but invisible in the gloom of their dingy nests.

My father had a pair of Glaremaster Goggles made especially for me when I was only twelve years old. I remember the long journey to the Glaremaster factory in the Midlands for my first fitting. It was during term time and I was given an absence chit to cover a number of school classes that I particularly disliked. The fitting process took nearly the whole day and started with a tour of the factory. My head was carefully measured and precise readings were taken of the color of my eyes and even the sensitivity of my skin. As part of the fitting service I was assigned a unique fitting reference number, and I remember being amazed when they told me that they would keep my details on their records for a hundred years.

My Glaremaster Goggles took nearly four months to make and I received them later that year as a special Christmas present. Over

STEP 7. Using a pair of kitchen scissors, carefully cut out the lenses.

STEP 8. To make the inner colored filters, cut two circles of hard candy wrapper cellophane (or similar) about the same size as the lenses. Check out whether you can see through the sheet by holding it close to your eyes; most candy wrappers and even some foil potato chip bags are actually see-through if you look up close.

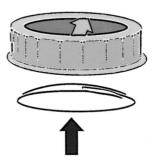

STEP 9. Assemble the eyepieces by first sticking the lens inside the golden ring. To do this, first put some glue inside the ring. If using glue-gun glue, wait a few seconds for it to cool slightly before pressing in the lens as the very hot glue can melt the lens slightly and spoil the look of it.

**STEP 10.** Next put a ring of glue on the goggle strap just around the eyehole and stick the color filter film to that.
Lastly apply some glue to the underside of the ring and stick that to the goggle strip.

**STEP 11.** Using a gold or silver marker, or a paintbrush, make a number of small dots along the goggle strip as shown on the template. Alternatively make up your own pattern.

**STEP 12.** Don't forget the Velcro (hook and loop fastener). Use a self-adhesive version, sew on, or stick on with glue-gun glue. Remember that the Velcro is stuck to the front of one end and the back of the other end so that the strap lies flat when the Velcro is fastened.

the years I took great care of my Glaremasters: I never replaced them, but I did occasionally send them back to the manufacturers to be serviced, or to have the strap lengthened or the bridge widened as I grew up.

Even now, in the twenty-first century, when there are no more dragons to vanquish, and in any case the hunting of them has become illegal, the goggles come in very handy for searching for things in the basement at night and occasionally for automobile driving on sunny days. In fact, I wear them whenever the situation permits and even occasionally when it doesn't. I love the rich smell of leather they exude and the sense of history I feel once I am in the grip in their protective caress. What is more, when I wear them in public, they never fail to attract the most admiring and covetous glances.

It's incredible to think that I have outlived those carefully maintained fitting records, but it also a sad fact that Glaremaster Limited, the company responsible for the manufacture of these amazing goggles all those years before, is no longer in business. However, don't give up hope. If you would like to own a pair, then although you will not be able to take a day off your school studies to travel across half the country with your father for a Glaremaster fitting, you will be able to make a pair of your own. I have taken the time and trouble to prepare some instructions for you to make a pair for yourself. Of course, it is likely that you will have to forego one or two of the Glaremaster's more advanced features, but the results are pleasing enough.

### Tracing templates

*Goggle outline*

*Trace onto paper.*
*Extend the ends to the correct length to fit around your head and then use to cut out the leather.*

*Lens cutting circle guide*

*Trace guide onto paper.*
*Cut out circle of the correct size to fit inside your bottle tops and then use it to draw an accurate circle on the shoulder of a 2-liter soda bottle.*

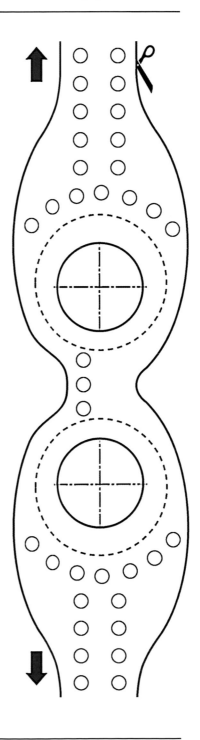

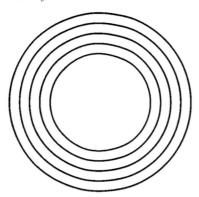

# Dragonesk Bottle Stopper

## A chance encounter with Le Comte de Saint-Germain

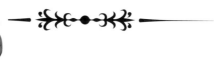

Although I never reveal my age, people are often puzzled at how I can look so young and yet be able to describe my adventurous activities of more than one hundred years ago as if the events were only a few weeks past. I can reveal however that I owe my longevity to a single brief encounter with **Le Comte de Saint-Germain**, whom I met by accident as I traveled across Europe on official business in the winter of 1898.

It is perhaps both my penance and my salvation that as an adventurer I must spend a great deal of my time in transit from one place to another. Due to the nature

*Parts templates*

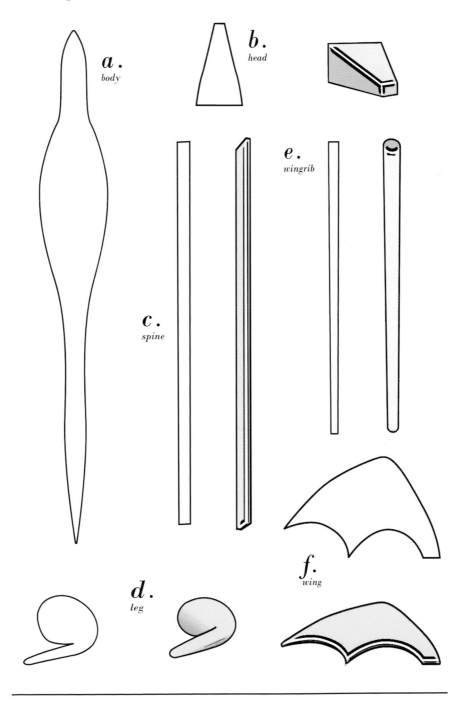

*a.*
body

*b.*
head

*e.*
wingrib

*c.*
spine

*f.*
wing

*d.*
leg

# Dragonesk Stopper

**STEP 1.** Using oven-bake clay such as Sculpey or Fimo, roll out and make the dragon component parts following the templates on the template page. When you have rolled or made the parts, lay them on the printed page and look directly down from above them; you should just not be able to see any of the template lines. Shutting one eye helps to see if the parts are lined up. To make the flat pieces roll out the clay using a pencil like a tiny rolling pin.

**STEP 2.** Take the leg part and bend the end around to make the foot and ankle joint. You don't need to pay too much attention to the foot detail because it is hidden in the finished model.

*head end*

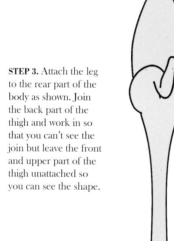

**STEP 3.** Attach the leg to the rear part of the body as shown. Join the back part of the thigh and work in so that you can't see the join but leave the front and upper part of the thigh unattached so you can see the shape.

*tail end*

of my business, my journeys often take me far from the beaten track, to places that are accessible only by the roughest modes of transport. On a good day I might find myself sharing a cramped cabin with the humblest of traveling companions; on a bad day I can be found making do with straw for warmth, in a rickety boxcar, shoulder to flank with gently swaying livestock giving me the evil eye. Nevertheless, it must be said that I always find pleasure in the journey, whatever the circumstances. Once in a while however, I am afforded the opportunity to travel in style. On one such occasion I had the delight of traveling by the charter of His Imperial Majesty, the Sultan of the Ottoman Empire, to facilitate some secret business, that I am not at liberty to reveal here, save to say that the trip afforded me the luxury of taking the newest and most fashionable means of transport of the day, the Orient Express.

The trip was wonderful and would have been perfect had it not been for the fact that I was suffering from a virulent cold and spent most of the first day confined to my couchette. By the evening I was feeling a bit better and thought that I should at least attempt an appearance at dinner. I made my way to the dining car and found that due to the tardiness of my arrival there were no free tables. I was about to return to my room when I was hailed by a gentleman sitting on his own. I approached his table and told him of my condition and said that I had made up my mind to forgo supper for fear of spreading the infection. Notwithstanding my protestations, the gentleman was insistent that I should stay. He told me that not only was he was immune to such diseases but that he was carrying a preparation in his luggage that would drive away my influenza within the hour, and leave me feeling as well as ever.

Without further ado we were introduced, and even before our hors d'œuvres had been served the Count had sent one of his footmen to his suite to retrieve a bottle of the preparation he so heartily swore by. When the footman returned, the Count urged me to take of the medicine (which to maintain

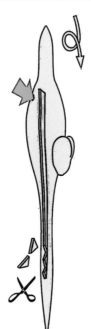

**STEP 4.** Turn the dragon over and attach the long flat strip c to the back along the spine, then using a pair of small (nail) scissors snip out Vs to make spikes.

**STEP 5.** Cut a scallop out of the head shape b then turn over and . . .

**STEP 6.** . . . pinch in the wedge to make the snout and make two slits for the eyes.

**STEP 7.** Thin out the crest gently between forefinger and thumb and then snip Vs into it to make the head crest spikes. Finish off with some small grooves, lined up with the spikes, made using a cocktail stick.

# Dragonesk Stopper

**STEP 8.** Attach the head to the neck, smoothing the two parts together underneath, so that the neck fits nicely into the cutout you made in Step 5.

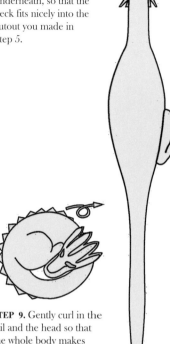

**STEP 9.** Gently curl in the tail and the head so that the whole body makes a circle. Tuck the foot under the head and the head under the tail.

**STEP 10.** Carefully turn over and, taking care not to squash the head or spikes, carefully cut a hole in the base at the center. Do not go all the way through. Cut the hole slightly bigger than the head of a 1 ¼-inch (30 mm) self-tapping wood screw.

his anonymity, he had called Chamberline's Longlife Linctus), without delay, and although unconvinced as to its efficacy I took a small draft of the bitter tasting syrup. Indeed it was fast acting; almost immediately I felt the color return to my cheeks. I offered to purchase the potion from him, but with a shake of the hand he refused, insisting instead that I keep the bottle "in case of other ailments" for which he claimed his so-called Universal Medicine would be more than a match. He leaned across the table and in hushed tones cautioned me to retain the curious little dragon-shaped stopper that decorated and sealed the top, for without it, he confided, the liquid would quickly lose its potency.

Over the course of our dinner together, I learned a great deal from this incredible man. I sat with wide eyes and slackened jaw as I listened, unbelieving, to the preposterous tale that he was already three hundred years old, even though by my best reckoning he did not look a day past his fortieth year. He pronounced at length that he had developed all manner of amazing things and wondrous techniques. The secret of Universal Medicine that was, it must be said, certainly making short work of my cold, was apparently among the most trifling of his inventions. He claimed that he possessed a mastery over nature and that he could melt diamonds: professing himself capable of forming, out of ten or twelve small diamonds, one large one of the most flawless purity and beauty, without any loss of weight. As you might imagine the evening passed quickly and most agreeably. After a formidable meal, I retired late, fully cured from my cold and not in the least bit tired. On my return from Constantinople, I placed the bottle in my safe, but since that journey I have not had occasion to use the prescription, nor, as I began to discover over the years that followed, have I aged significantly. I have at various times attempted to extract the ingredients that make up this incredible cure-all, by use of tincture and distillation, using the merest droplets of the priceless liquid in my experiments, but I have had no luck whatsoever,

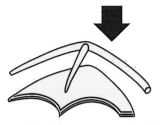

**STEP 11.** Attach the spar part e to the wing flap f, as shown above, taking care to keep the form of the spar.

**STEP 12.** Attach the wing underneath and at the back and blend in the join at the top of the wing, by the shoulder. To give the impression of scales, press the edge of a knife gently against the tail in a crisscross pattern.

**STEP 13.** Following the instructions for your oven-bake modeling clay, bake the dragon for about 15 to 20 minutes. Rest it on a china or glass egg cup and pull the tip of the tail down slightly.

# Dragonesk Stopper

**STEP 14.** While the dragon is baking hard, prepare the cork. Carefully shave off slices all the way around to make it tapered; lots of little slices to keep it smooth, but finish off with sandpaper for a really smooth finish.

**STEP 15.** Screw a medium sized self tapping screw 1 ¼" (30 mm) into the center of the cork so that it pokes up enough to fit inside the dragon hole that you made in Step 10.

**STEP 16.** After baking, let the dragon cool and spray with silver paint. For a really good finish when the spray is almost dry coat in silver leaf, then buff. To age it, paint it with black acrylic paint and wipe it off before it is dry, thereby leaving some in all the creases.

**STEP 17.** When the paint has dried, polish up the silver and detail the eye in red paint. Finally mix up some epoxy resin or strong glue and glue the dragon to the cork so that the screw is glued into the hole underneath it.

and the contents of that incredible bottle remain a mystery to me even to this day.

Unfortunately I am therefore not able to offer you a recipe for the formulation of the amazing Universal Medicine. Nevertheless I am able to present to you instructions on how to fabricate the elegant dragon-shaped bottle stopper that by all accounts maintains the liquid's unique properties.

# Dragon Scales

## And the manufacture of artificial ones for your private collection

The uses for dragon scales are far too numerous to mention. Lighter than titanium, harder than diamond, but as tough and flexible as rubber, dragonite is one of nature's finest achievements and always took the place of man-made materials in applications where its unique properties were required and the installation cost could be justified.

For some people, however, despite their formidable properties dragon scales merely serve a decorative purpose. Often they are to be found in prominent positions, proudly displayed in cabinets or shadow boxes on withdrawing room walls up and down the Country, acting as status symbols or tangible proof of successful hunting campaigns. For the more boastful of those who hunt for sport, smaller scales may be strung on short lengths of twine and worn around the neck or wrist, much as

**STEP 1.** Make your dragon scales with authentic soft curves easily by using the curved edges of any kitchen or personal care product bottle. The bottle material is tough, stiff, and lightweight, just like a real dragon scale.

**STEP 2.** Using the template in this chapter as a guide, or making up your own shape, mark out the shape of your dragon scale so that it straddles the corner of a plastic bottle, or right over the top shoulder for a really curvy scale.

**STEP 3.** Carefully and neatly cut out the scale shape using a pair of strong kitchen scissors. You should be able to cut quite a few from a single bottle; wash off the marker with soap and water and kitchen scouring pad.

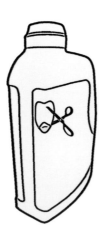

a native from the Southern Seas might wear a trophy necklace of shark's teeth or porcupine quills. Barons Manor has an extensive collection of scales with at least one example from every known dragon as well as a few from creatures that have yet to be formally identified. I hope you don't think it immodest of me when I tell you that, in fact, the Barons' dragon scale collection is widely considered to be one of the finest in the world. I hasten to add, mind you, that because I have never hunted the beasts with the intention of killing them, the collection is made up purely of those scales that I have found discarded in the proximity of the various dragon nests and holes that I have encountered on my travels, or from animals that died of natural causes.

However they may have been collected, dragon scales certainly do make entertaining pieces, and their beautiful symmetry and iridescent color never fails to delight the eye of even the most scientific observer. For this reason display grade scales were always been in high demand, and by the early 1900s the buying and selling of dragon scales dominated every country's dragonolia trade.

As a result, there was an outcry when the trade in dragon materials and artifacts was prohibited in the 1930s. The ban was not all bad news though, because when the manufacture of artificial dragonolia began in earnest I was able to put the Barons Manor workshop to good use in order to supply a market hungry for firebelly products. Within a few short years a booming traffic developed for all manner of man-made dragonry products, and the Barons Brand became world famous for quality and unsurpassed refinement. But by far the most successful of all our products were our beautiful man-made dragon scales.

We developed two methods for making them. The first was a most expensive and time-consuming process, and involved growing the scales from a bath of minerals. The second, a rather simpler and cheaper method (although somewhat inferior), involved a process of casting them from a specially prepared beetle wing-cover paste.

The artificial scales grown using our patented process from a special bath of mineral salts were perfect in

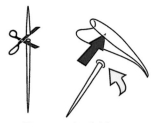

**STEP 4.** To get a perfect finish on your scale you will need it to be held while you spray it. To hold it properly, cut the tip off a cocktail stick and glue the cut end onto the back of the scale.

**STEP 5.** Hold the dragon scale in place by poking the cocktail stick into an egg carton or something similar. For an authentic leathery texture on the scale, stick a piece of leather to the plastic and trim off to the plastic edge before spraying.

**STEP 6.** Paint the scale with waterproof paint. Spray paint will give the best finish. Use more than one color to get a nice graded effect. Leave the cocktail stick on if you want to display your dragon scales in a box frame.

every way. The process was an immediate success and scales made using this method easily fooled even the most experienced dragonologist.

Mineral grown scales had all the qualities of the originals and were every bit as beautiful as those from which they were copied. In those days, they were prized as fashion accessories or items of jewelry, and even today (although it is not widely known) they have various interesting and secret military uses due to their complete resistance to bullet penetration and utter invisibility under the scrutiny of radar.

Unfortunately, mineral grown scales are also very, very expensive, more so even than diamonds. As a result I quickly found that most customers simply could not afford the luxury of owning a mineral grown scale. It was for these customers that we developed the simpler cast scale process. In many cases, customers housing private collections found that our simpler and more cost-effective dragon scale manufacturing process produced a more than acceptable result for their purposes.

Mind you, the cast scale process was still rather involved and began with the use of a mortise and pestle to crush of thousands of black beetle carapaces by hand into a fine dust. The valuable dust was then collected and mixed with a special solvent that could dissolve the beetle chitin and create a thick, quick-setting liquid paste that could be cast or molded into curved dragon scale–shaped sheets, ready to be coated in the relevant color. Unlike authentic or mineral grown dragon scales, the scales produced by this process are not heatproof, so in order to color them a cold enamel must be used. The result is still highly attractive and enduring.

Neither process is practiced today, and knowing that you may well have problems locating a sufficient supply of beetle carapaces, I have devised a simple third process for which I have drawn up some straightforward plans. The diligent student will be able to make their very own replica dragon scales using materials that can be found in most modern homes. I trust you will use this information wisely, and when you have the time, make a fine collection of scales to adorn your walls and impress your houseguests whenever they visit.

### Dragon scale templates

*And the names given to scales of these forms, each given to a particular species of dragon.*

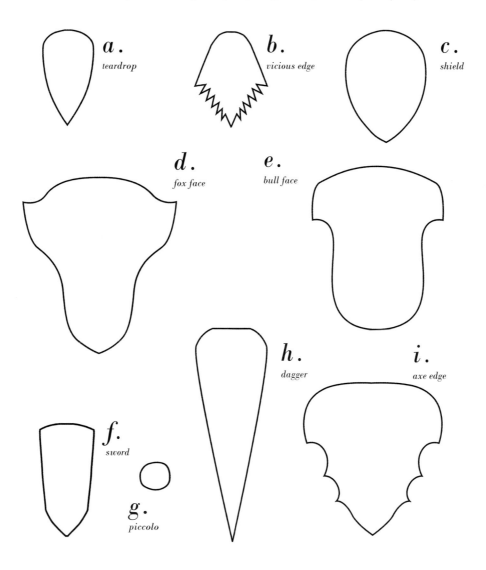

**a.** teardrop

**b.** vicious edge

**c.** shield

**d.** fox face

**e.** bull face

**f.** sword

**g.** piccolo

**h.** dagger

**i.** axe edge

# Wizard's Wand

## The big freeze of '27

The winter of 1927 was one of the coldest in living memory. Snow fell heavily all over England, and many people remained trapped in their homes for weeks on end. On Salisbury Plain the snow lay so deep that it obscured Stonehenge, drifting as high as twenty feet in places. Unfortunately it was also the year that our generally efficient heating system faltered, and the normally welcoming atmosphere of Barons Manor became decidedly Siberian. Various pipes froze and long icicle chandeliers formed dangerously from the light fittings in most of the larger rooms. Our heating system was by no means traditional. In those days our boiler was not the more usual oil-fired contraption of dials, pumps, and copper tubing that you might expect, but a Welsh dragon called Angeline that I had rescued from poachers over thirty years before. It may not surprise you to learn, therefore, that the nature of its failure and its subsequent repair was no less extraordinary.

I discovered Angeline on a remote Welsh mountainside as near to death as it is possible for a living thing to be. It's probable that the poachers who killed her mother had left the dragon chick for dead because she was too small to be of any value to them. However, it was immediately clear to me that she had been gravely injured and without her mother her chances of survival in the wild were nonexistent. Though the fire in her belly was cool to the touch, her eyes were ablaze with fighting spirit, and I decided to take her back with me in the hope that I could nurse her back to health. The fact that I had no training in the veterinary science did not deter me; dragons aren't like any normal beast, and so I reasoned that I had as good a chance as anyone of breathing life back into the poor bedraggled creature. I cut short my trip and made haste back to England. As soon as I was back, I had a small, clean nest made in the basement and made the dragonette as comfortable as I could. Angeline (as she had quickly become known) responded well to my ministrations, and before a year had passed, the little dragon was doing well and growing quickly. It was with a heavy heart that the following summer I released her back in to the wild in Gwynedd, close to where we had found her the previous year.

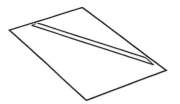

**STEP 1.** Stick a strip of double-sided tape diagonally across and sheet of letter-size paper.

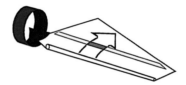

**STEP 2.** Roll the paper up very tightly diagonally, allowing one end to be slightly less tight than the other to give a thin tapered roll.

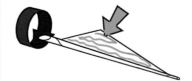

**STEP 3.** When you roll over the double-sided tape, stop and put a little white glue on the remaining paper.

**STEP 4.** Roll the rest of the paper tightly and leave to dry for 30 minutes.

**STEP 5.** Trim to give straight ends.

**STEP 6.** Fill each end with glue-gun glue, one end at a time. Pack the bigger end with tissue if you want to use less glue-gun glue. The bigger end might take two or three goes to completely fill it.

We neither saw nor heard anything of Angeline for months, so it was quite a shock when, one October morning, we woke to find her curled up asleep on the back terrace, glowing warmly and snorting with contentment. Up until then little had been known about wyverns, but it quickly became apparent that they hibernate each year and that Angeline had chosen to return to Barons Manor to snooze away the snowy months somewhere she felt secure. I had the doorway to the cellar widened and she wasted no time in slithering down into the basement where she stayed for the rest of the winter.

Year after year Angeline returned. Each year the cellar door and stairway needed enlarging, and each year Angeline's glowing body kept Barons Manor as warm as toast through the inclement months. Such was the efficiency and reliability of this strangely ecological system that I let the original heating apparatus fall into disrepair.

As I have already mentioned 1927 was a very cold winter and that particular year Angeline arrived late. She had taken to coming for her hibernation at the beginning of October, and toward the end of the month when she had not appeared, I found myself spending an hour or so each evening anxiously searching the skies for her familiar form. The house grew colder and colder with each passing day. The staff complained bitterly, but I hardly noticed the cold as I became increasingly worried that perhaps the poachers had finally caught up with her. By November I feared the worst and sent one of the Manor staff up to Gwynedd to see if they could find any news of the dragon. No news was forthcoming, and I had all but given up hope when one night in December, after the first snow had fallen, I was woken by a loud crashing sound that rattled the windows and shook the house to its foundations. I dressed quickly and ran out into the night followed by the rest of the household that had been similarly roused. There, right next to the house, scrunched up in a tangled ball, like a smoldering boulder at the end of a long dark scar, gouged in the snow-covered lawn, lay Angeline, crying like a kitten and catching her breath in short fitful pants.

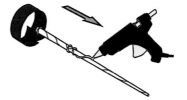

**STEP 7.** Apply a glue-gun bead on the outside of the wand while turning the wand to make a nice pattern. Keep turning it while the glue sets (about 1 minute).

**STEP 8.** Spray the wand with an undercoat of latex paint to seal.

**STEP 9.** Paint wand with base color of your choice. Use acrylic paint that dries permanent. The painting doesn't have to be very even.

**STEP 10.** When the base coat is dry, start painting with a thinned wash off black acrylic paint, making sure that the black gets into all the little cracks.

**STEP 11.** As you are painting, wipe of the paint with a damp paper towel to leave dark paint in the cracks and corners.

**STEP 12.** Rub some gold paint, burnishing paste, or gold gel marker onto the raised beads to highlight them.

She was too weak to walk on her own, but with ropes and pulleys and some help from the local farmer's draft horses, we managed to drag her gently down into the safety of the basement. Once inside the building and under proper illumination it was clear that the beautiful dragon was very badly injured. This time it was obvious that nothing short of a miracle would be enough to make her well again. We made her as comfortable as we could and I retired to the library to begin the search for some clues as to what might be done.

After days of frantic searching at I found an ancient magical text describing an enchantment guaranteed to heal a dragon, but only if it was performed with a wand made from part of the dragon itself. I explained the situation as well as I was able to the dying Angeline, and although she cried out in pain, I think she understood what I was doing as I cut away enough of her wing-web to make the small wand. I rolled the skin tightly into a wand, gluing it with ant saliva and binding it with spider silk. I wasted no time in getting it to work, immediately pointing it at Angeline and reciting the incantation I had earlier memorized. The second I had uttered the last word, thick silken threads gushed from the tip of the wand, pushing me back with such force that I was very nearly thrown off my feet. I stood my ground however, and the sparkling filaments fizzed, flying around the dragon and cocooning her in a thick layer of shining silk.

Angeline stayed wrapped in her chrysalis overcoat for the rest of the winter. We dared not fire up the mechanical heating system for fear of disturbing her. That winter of 1927 we froze, but when the spring came and the dragon imago emerged perfectly healed, yawned, and lazily spread her golden wings, as if nothing had ever been wrong with her, the icy months were forgotten.

For sentimental reasons I was unable to destroy the wand even though it had served its purpose. Since that day I have kept it securely locked in a charm proof box, and am glad to say that I have never had cause to use it again.

However, when compiling these notes, it occurred to me that you might also like the opportunity of making a wand for your own purposes. Of course, I appreciate that you may not have a distressed dragon on your hands, and your supply of ant saliva or spider silk might be somewhat limited. Nevertheless, a very credible wand may be fashioned, in an almost identical manner to the one I employed, by the use of writing paper, white glue, and hot-melt adhesive. I trust you will find these instructions adequate for the purpose.

# Aurified Dragon Embryo

## And how I made my greatest discovery by mistake

B efore I was even born, way back when dragons were a common sight in our skies, the trade in dragon-related artifacts was slow. With the exception of rare and therefore highly prized items, which occasionally turned up in the better auction houses and fetched quite sizable sums, it must be said that ordinary dragon articles were considered as no more than pretty novelties. By the turn of the twentieth century, dragonolia had become popular and shops began to spring up everywhere, offering a wide range of dragon-related products.

Of course, wealthy and discerning collectors were never interested in buying cheap firebelly products in the average dragonry; rich collectors always wanted something special. This was of course to my good fortune, and I was continuously employed by Europe's richest families, whose desire to own the impossible was only matched by their incredible resources to pay for the most daring and expensive expeditions. However, during World War II, I decided to take a break from hunting down priceless dragonolia and temporarily evacuated Barons Manor to safer lands, where to my astonishment I made one of my greatest discoveries of my life, and completely by accident!

Since the beginning of the war, I had kept a low profile, for despite my spritely step and youthful look (courtesy of Chamberline's Longlife Linctus), and numerous decorations for valor in the Great War twenty-five years earlier, I had been excused army service on account of my age. After all, it is hardly dignified nor expected of a gentleman of over ninety years to be taking up arms. When the bombing came too close for comfort, I closed up the house and took myself and my staff to the safety of a remote Tibetan monastery, where I planned to write and develop a few of my inventions until the war was over.

During that time I kept up my interest in dragon paraphernalia, and with the help of some willing locals began the scientific study of what I now

**STEP 1.** Roll out your Fimo or Sculpey modeling clay or air-dry clay, so that it fits over the template shapes on the template page at the end of this project.

**STEP 2.** To make the forelegs, bend the relevant rolled out pieces of clay to make a Z shape.

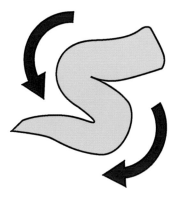

**STEP 3.** To make the hind legs, bend the relevant rolled out pieces of clay to make an S shape.

**STEP 4.** Attach the legs to the body as shown, blending them in at upper end only. Don't worry too much about foot detail, as the feet will be hidden by the curl of the tail. Flatten the eyes slightly and attach, then make a slit in them to make the eyelids using a dinner knife. Attach the crest to the top of the head.

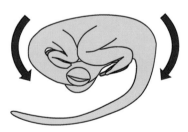

**STEP 5.** Taking care not to crush the model, carefully bend the head around and tuck between the forelegs and hind legs. Also bend the tail around.

**STEP 6.** Curl the tail around in a neat spiral and loop over the base of the tail. Blend some of the clay into the body, but make sure you keep the definition between tail and body. Use a cocktail stick to make detail.

know to be the last breeding pair of Tibetan lungs anywhere in the world. The days were long and although the mountainous countryside was stark it was wildly beautiful. The monastery was free of the whine of mechanical equipment as the monks preferred to live a simple life. A sparse but nourishing diet was maintained solely from local produce, and even our water, cool and pure, was drawn from the monastery's own well. While I was there I wrote notes about some of my previous adventures and started to draw up the pictures that would later be used in this very book. Like the dragons that fascinate me, I too am a bit of a hoarder, and I collected oddments from the locality that took my fancy and after a year or two had amassed a reasonable assortment of interesting artifacts. Among them, a beautiful egg-shaped stone stood out as a most intriguing item. I had the strongest feeling that its smooth, shimmering surface concealed some ancient inner secret, but I lacked the courage to break it open for fear of destroying its immeasurable beauty. One day, fate took the decision out of my hands, when quite by accident, in a moment of carelessness, I knocked it, and being round, it rolled off the table where I had been studying it only moments earlier. It cracked with a sickening thud on the flagstone floor. When I picked it up, the smooth surface seemed to crumble in my hand, exposing a perfectly formed golden dragon embryo. Even as I looked at it, I knew that I was beholding something that perhaps no man had ever seen. I am not ashamed to admit that not only did my hand shake as I placed the piece gently back on the table, but I even glanced furtively over my shoulder to make absolutely certain that no one had seen what had happened. While the filigree egg case might be rare, up until that point, golden (or aurified) dragon embryos were thought to have only existed in myths. The exhaustive research I have conducted since has revealed that there has been only one other known example, and that one was lost in the firestorm that destroyed the Great Library of Alexandria in 48 BC.

Needless to say, I made no mention of my extraordinary find to anyone, fearing that it might be

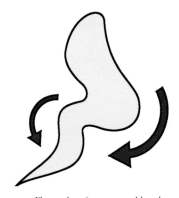

**STEP 7.** Flatten the wing parts and bend into an elongated Z shape.

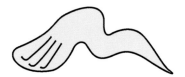

**STEP 8.** Flatten out the thicker end some more and make a few small markings in the top to represent the half formed wing detail.

**STEP 9.** Join the wings to the back of the dragon embryo, blending it in, in a couple of places.

**STEP 10.** If you have used normal, air-dry clay, allow the clay to dry until it is hard. If you have used oven-bake clay, follow the oven baking instructions. Usually this will be to bake for about 20 minutes on the lowest heat. Support the model carefully so that it doesn't squash or droop while it is baking.

**STEP 11.** Allow to cool; run under cold water to speed up the cooling process. Then spray or paint the embryo with gold paint.

**STEP 12.** When the first layer of paint has dried, distress the piece if you want. To distress, paint a coat of slightly watered-down black acrylic paint over the whole of the piece, making sure to paint in all the cracks and creases. Before the paint dries wipe with a damp paper towel so that the black paint stays in all the cracks and creases. When dry polish up with black wax shoe polish for an authentic antique look.

stolen from me or that I might be prohibited from taking back to England. I carefully wrapped the piece in two ten-srang banknotes and buried it in one of my numerous luggage compartments. Each night for the next two years, when no one was about, I took the small icon from its hiding place and studied it under a magnifying glass by dim light of the crude oil lamp that was the monastery's sole form of night-time illumination. How had it become aurified? Why was this process so rare? How old was the piece?

In 1945 we returned to England, and since then, whenever my schedule permits, I have searched for an answer to these three questions. Nevertheless, such is the rarity of the piece, that after even sixty-five years of diligent research, my queries remain totally unanswered. Perhaps you can help. I have drawn some simple directions, which should enable you to make a faithful copy of the tiny golden dragon embryo. Once you have done so, you might study it yourself and gain an insight that has escaped my endeavours. I look forward to hearing from you.

# My Greatest Discovery

## Embryo templates

These templates have been designed to be easy to use and are all based on rolling out different shaped sausages of oven-bake clay such as Fimo or Sculpey. To use the templates, roll out your clay so that when you place it over the template when looking from directly above the piece you can see a tiny bit of the outline all around the edge. Bend, fold, and flatten the pieces as described on the project instructions, and then join them to the body to make your dragon embryo.

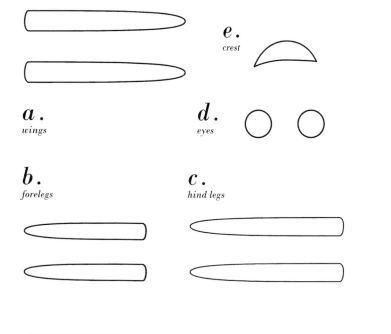

***f.***
*body*

***e.***
*crest*

***a.***
*wings*

***d.***
*eyes*

***b.***
*forelegs*

***c.***
*hind legs*

# Dreamcatcher

## Gorgeous creatures and golden dreams

In her sixteenth year, Lottie, my great-niece, received a blow to the head when she fell from her horse while out riding, and as a result suffered from the most distressing nightmares that thereafter prevented her from getting any restful sleep. All manner of physicians were consulted, and despite the combined efforts of some of the best medical quackery in the land, no relief could be found. After two years of broken nights and tearful days her parents were at their wits' end and Lottie was all but confined to her bed, weak as she was from her inability to sleep in it. I felt I had to do something to help and searched the Barons' library for any clue that might point the way to a potential cure for her distressing malady. After months of reading all manner of unrewarding texts, one morning I chanced upon a slim and dusty but otherwise untarnished book, called *Celestial Beings from the In-Between and Other Gorgeous Creatures*. It described the elusive dragon spirit, a well-known New World cure for terrors of the dark hours. Further reading revealed that tales of such spirits originated from Brazil, and so not wanting to waste another second, I took the six o'clock train down to Southampton and chartered a flight direct to Ilha de Marajó (eel-ha de Mar-a-ho), the world's largest freshwater island, in the mouth of the mighty Amazon river.

When one considers an island in the mouth of a river, one thinks of a small scrap of land that might be traversed on foot in the course of a morning, but I must tell you that Marajó is the size of Switzerland and the particular settlement I sought was many miles from the city of Breves where I disembarked after my arduous flight. Add to this the fact that island is rather underdeveloped and has no roads to speak of, and you may not be surprised to learn that my final destination was another

**STEP 1.** Cut a coat hanger carefully with a pair of pliers.

**STEP 2.** Straighten out the wire strip with the pliers. This makes it easier to make a nice circular hoop.

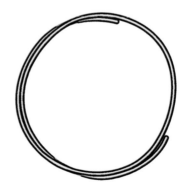

**STEP 3.** Fashion the wire into a circular hoop shape. Use the pliers to twist the wire around itself and use sticky tape to hold the wire to itself. Once you have a shape that won't spring apart you can work on it to make it as circular as possible.

two days' buffalo ride away. I booked into the city's best hotel and considered the final leg of my journey.

The library in Breves provided more information on the habits and habitats of dragon spirits. Dragon spirits are delicate and particularly susceptible to injury from magnetism or electrical fields, and Marajó is one of the last natural habitats of this elusive creature. Due to the enormous outpouring of the Amazon, Marajó island is regularly swamped by flooding and as a result the locals build their houses on stilts. It is this precarious construction, combined with the island's remoteness, that has provided the perfect environment for dragon spirits to flourish. Apparently, a suitably trained observer may just be able to glimpse the ethereal spirits playing in the shady reflections that dance off the languid freshwater pools found in the spaces under Marajó's elevated dwellings.

The buffalo ride out to the remote village was much more comfortable than I had expected, but due to the lack of burden cattle available, I was forced to leave the bulk of my equipment behind and was only permitted to take the most essential supplies: a reasonably compact traveling wardrobe with lightweight wire coat hangers, a cut down library of only forty books or so, and a delicate pottery jar. I planned to use the jar to capture and store the dream spirit, and had wrapped it carefully in the soft feather pillow I was taking as my gift offering to the village shaman, whose I help I would certainly need if I was to study and capture a spirit. It was dusk as our small procession entered the village. Far as we were from any form of artificial illumination, the night drew implacably over us like a velvet blanket as the forest rang with the howls and whoops of a million animals, chattering in anticipation of the pitch-black Amazonian night.

The shaman, who permitted no lamps in his home, gracefully received my gift, although when he hung it on the wall of his hut I was not entirely sure that he fully understood its purpose. He sat perfectly still in the gathering gloom and raised my hopes by telling me tales of the various different types of dragon spirits and how they were all descended from Yemanja (yeh-man-jar), the ocean mother and protector of all children. However, my hopes were dashed by his raucous laughter at my idea of capturing a spirit and taking it home to cure Lottie of her nightmares. Once his laughter had subsided he casually dismissed my idea with a wave of his hand.

"Dragon spirits bring us dreams," he told me in the quaint mixture of Portuguese and sign language he had been using to tell his stories. "They cannot be captured and kept in a jar any more than you can catch an idea and keep it in a box."

I didn't show my disappointment; instead, over the course of the next hour, I persuaded him to train me to become aware of the spirits so that might I learn more about them and thus determine for myself the best course of action. That night I retired exhausted and had the most vivid dreams filled with golden-scaled caiman, yellow-beaked toucans, and pink river dolphins.

Over the weeks that followed under the shaman's guidance, I learned many curious things about the ghostly dragons. I learned that while some dragon spirits are visible, others only exist as sounds, and yet others are noticeable only as smells or fleeting tastes. The shaman also taught me the technique of daydreaming—not the idle slack-jawed state of the typical student in a schoolroom on a hot summer's afternoon, but the purposeful, heightened state of awareness that lets one see and communicate with the spirits whenever one wishes. He taught me how to use a reflection as a window into the spirit world. He explained that reflected light provides a gentler form of illumination that is more capable of revealing the delicate form of the spirits. Of course, the people of the forest have never seen a looking glass, so they use the surface of water as their reflective medium. I practiced all day until I could see the spirits whenever I tried and then went back to my room to

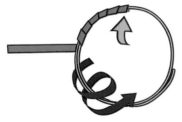

**STEP 4.** Wrap the hoop in a thin fabric or leather so that no metal is showing. Glue the strip at the beginning with glue-gun glue and then every so often as you wrap it around.

**STEP 5.** To make the web, use about 6 1/2 feet (2 m) of thin string. Tie it tightly round the hoop in one place, then loop it at intervals round the edge of the hoop until you have about 6 to 8 points where the strip loops round the hoop. Make sure that you pull the string really tight and keep it tight as you go around.

**STEP 6.** When you get all the way around the hoop and near the original knot, instead of looping the string around the hoop, loop it around the middle of the first string span and pull tight. After a couple of loops in the string, thread a brightly colored bead onto the string.

try out my new skill on the mirror that hung on the inside of my wardrobe. When I opened the cupboard door I was shocked to see that moths had eaten all my best suits. But when I stared into the mirror I saw in its reflection that inside each of my now otherwise empty wire coat hangers a golden dragon spirit ducked and swam as if trapped in a fisherman's net. I reached in to retrieve a hanger and in doing so touched one of them with the cuff of my shirt. The spirit in that hanger leapt free, circling madly around the room for a few seconds before disappearing through the floor into the forest below. After some considerable experimentation I found that the best shape for containing the spirits was a circular hoop wound with fabric or thin strips of leather. The effect was further enhanced by the presence of a simple net or web, woven across the hoop. I found also that the spirits might be set free by the use of yarn, feathers, or fabric decorations that, when hung from the contraption, allowed the spirit to escape the hoop's magnetic grip. The shaman was impressed by what he called my dreamcatcher and finally, after nearly thirty-five days on Marajó, I was ready to make my way back to England. With extreme care I carried the spirit-laden dreamcatcher back in my hand luggage, holding it whenever possible, glancing in any passing window or reflective surface to make sure that the dragon spirits captured inside it were still there.

As soon as I got back to England I wasted no time in going to Lottie's house. I instructed her parents to hang the dreamcatcher above her bed and decorate it with feathers so that as the night came the beautiful dragon spirits might escape and flow over her so she might finally sleep and dream in the gentle caress of the dragon spirits.

As far as I know, that night, Lottie slept for twelve hours, dreaming of golden-scaled caiman, yellow-beaked toucans, and pink river dolphins, and to this day has never had another nightmare.

Should you wish to make your own dreamcatcher, I hope you will be able to avoid a lengthy and expensive trip to South America by using these simple instructions.

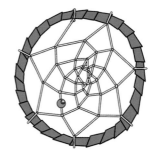

**STEP 7.** Continue around the circle, looping the string around the middle of each of the string spans of the previous pass, and just keep going until you only have a small hole left in the center. Tie off the string in a final knot.

**STEP 8.** Decorate your dreamcatcher with personal trinkets. Make three tassels to hang from your dreamcatcher.

**STEP 9.** Tie the tassel strings on to the dreamcatcher hoop, one on each side and one at the bottom. Tie an extra piece of string to the top and hang your dreamcatcher on your bedpost or in your bedroom, near or over your bed. Sweet dreams!

# Apothecary Labels

## And a cure for mediocrity, humdrumience, and indifference

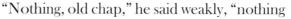

I t was with disbelief I sat at Monty's bedside on that bright autumn afternoon and stared into his pale vacant eyes, his face as long as a flapper's necklace.

"Nothing, old chap," he said weakly, "nothing at all. Go on, ask me another." Dutifully I obliged.

"Who captained the English side for the first test played at Trent Bridge in 1899?"

Monty's face stared blankly out at me, but all he could muster was, "I have no idea old chap, not a sausage; my mind is completely blank." I turned to the housekeeper and asked if the doctor had been called, but before she could answer, Monty struggled up on one arm and leaned close to me, agitated at the mention of the doctor.

"Don't let that quack in here," he croaked, and then, glancing at the housekeeper, leaning even closer to me, and lowering his voice to a whisper; "do me a favor, old chap. You couldn't just pop down to Crumsbeak and Purdy in Old Compton Street, could you? I trust them, they'll know what to do." He flopped back on to the bed, apparently exhausted from the exertion. I found it impossible to reject such an earnest request and after a brief discussion with the housekeeper, where I learned further that Monty had been listless for two days and quite unlike himself. He had not been able to tell any funny stories, make any double entendres, or quote a single pointless fact on *any* topic. It was quickly agreed that I should go down to the apothecary, but if their remedy proved to be ineffectual by the evening, I would take it upon myself to call the doctor that night for an emergency consultation.

FULLY PREPARED

**Dragon Heartstring**

May be ground or powdered and mixed 2 parts to 1 part with angel tears for the treatment of Timidity, Tremulousness and excessive humility. Only to be administered by a Physician

Distributed by

**Crumsbeak & Purdy**

Prepared under licence

\* \* \*

Back in the 1920s one of my best friends was Viscount Montague Brassington-Smythe. He was so charming and respected by so many, that I felt honored to be counted amongst his closest confidantes.

He was a consummate host and threw legendary parties. Generous to a fault, a gifted pianist, an excellent bridge partner, bon vivant, and a wicked raconteur, Monty (as he was known to his closest friends) was, above everything else, the font of a vast quantity of facts and snippets of inconsequential information, blessed as he was with an unparalleled hunger for obscure tidbits of trivia and an agile mind that had been filled to the brim by an expensive education. It should therefore come as no surprise to the reader that he made an excellent traveling companion, and being about as tough as an old boot and as resourceful as a rook, had accompanied me on some of my most arduous expeditions. Knowing this then, I trust that you will be as distressed as I was, when I found myself making my way with some urgency from my good friend's London pied-à-terre to a quaint little chemist in Old Compton Street, WC1, with the hope of curing him of the mysterious malaise that had robbed him of his creativity and worst of all, his endearing penchant for making hilarious puns and the quoting of inconsequential facts on any subject.

* * *

I found the shop easily enough. Inside it was as dry as an autumn leaf and although some sunlight did force its way through the hazy windowpanes, what little did failed miserably in its attempt to illuminate the interior. With my eyes still adjusting to the gloom, I groped my way toward the counter. A strange assortment of bottles and jars crowded every available surface. I ran my eye along one of the dusty shelves. Goblin Ganglion "For the encouragement of Extravagance, Luxurious Exaggeration and Improvident Overindulgence"; Worm Ducts "For the treatment of Sickening Jolt, Tenderised Filaments and Necrotic Bulbasore"; and even Dragon Heartstring "For the treatment of Timidity, Tremulousness and Excessive Humility"; strange concoctions indeed, for even stranger sounding afflictions. At the back

of the apothecary, a tall and wiry fellow stood quietly behind the shop's only service counter. I made my way through the corridor of creaking display cases and politely greeted him. He said nothing, only nodding sagely as I related the events of the day and tried my best to describe the details of Monty's affliction and how the disease that ravaged him was robbing him of his unique qualities. He smiled and without a word, reached below the counter and produced a sheet of paper upon which were printed an assortment of labels exactly like the ones I had seen on the bottles lining the shelves. I waited for him to prepare one of his amazing concoctions, but instead he said the most curious thing.

"Take this sheet and get the patient to make up some of the potions. Cut out the labels from this sheet to make up some authentic looking apothecary preparations. It will be messy, and so it would be advisable if you were to wear old clothes or at the very least a splash-apron." By the quizzical look on my face, the shopkeeper could see that I was perplexed, but without pause, he continued.

"Take some old jars and long thin bottles and soak off the labels." From under the counter he took out an old shoe box, within which were a hodgepodge of old jam jars, small olive-oil bottles and old spice jars.

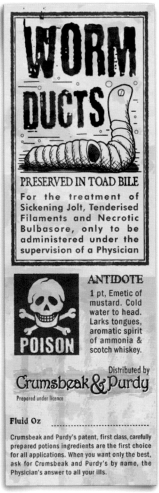

"I'm afraid you can't have these jars, as they are my samples," he continued, "but your housekeeper should be able to find something similar."

He put the jars away. "If you don't have wax to seal the top, carve an old cork and then cover it with hot melt glue, which you may then paint red to look like wax."

I could hold back no longer. "But what about the actual potions?" I bleated somewhat desperately.

"Use anything you have at hand," he replied, his face the picture of seriousness. "Jelly sweets floating in dessert jelly swell up nicely and look just like Worm Ducts; or you might try bread sticks or perhaps cinnamon sticks, as I am told they look just like Petrified Griffin Bone; or you may well find that sugar laces, licorice ropes, or even red wool yarn strands will be easily mistaken for Dragon Heartstrings."

He put his hands together and looked at me expectantly, with his eyebrows slightly raised; I was stunned to silence for a moment.

"B-b-but," I stuttered, "surely ingesting any of our own homemade potions would be ineffectual and there is the distinct possibility it could be dangerous, or that it even might complicate the patient's condition."

"You are not meant to *take* the ingredients," he snorted. "The prescription for your patient's condition is to engage in some purposeful creative activity." He turned the sheet around and pointing to the bottom of it said, "I'd start with the Polyp of Symbioslugella, that's the cure for mediocrity, humdrumience, and uninspiring indifference. I find that picked gherkins are almost identical to the genuine preparation."

As I walked back to the house, I had my reservations about the nature of the treatment, but later that evening, after we had made at least eight containers' worth of different potions and had what was starting to look like our very own apothecary, I looked at Monty standing at the kitchen table, grinning from ear to ear, shirtsleeves rolled up jauntily, carefully sticking an Antler Velvet label onto a jar of cut up red felt pieces, I knew at once that that wise old shopkeeper had been right—this was the perfect cure for boredom and ennui.

"W. G. Grace," Monty said out of the blue.

"I beg your pardon?"

"W. G. Grace! Captain of the English side for the first test played at Trent Bridge in 1899. He was an outstanding all-rounder, excelling at all the essential skills of batting, bowling, and fielding. But it is for his batting that he was most renowned as he is held to have invented modern batting. He was particularly noted for his mastery of all strokes, and this level of expertise has been said by all the most respected reviewers to be unique."

"Ahh, I see," I said, "that's interesting." The old Montague Brassington-Smythe I knew was back.

Should you wish to try your hand at a touch of potion making, you'll be glad to know that you don't have to go down to Old Compton Street to get antique apothecary labels. I have collected a few labels together and they are available for your use on www.dragonolia.com, especially for your enjoyment and of course for the alleviation of boredom the moment it strikes.

# Dragon Egg Pendant

## And the trouble with dragon imps

Each morning after breakfast, I set aside two hours to attend to my postbag. I call it "my armchair adventuring," because never a day goes by when I am not somehow transported to a distant realm by the opening of an envelope or interesting looking package, the contents of which take me on a voyage of discovery and rapture, all in the comfort of my own study, and even before the luncheon gong has sounded. However, occasionally something truly special lands on my desk that grabs my attention so fully as to utterly banish any thought of eating and all the duties planned for the remainder of the day. On one such occasion, about a year ago now, I received an unassuming letter from an experienced explorer called Melrose. The letter contained four miniature-dragon's eggs that, although they looked harmless enough, had caused her some considerable problems. She had disguised them as pendants, but when that failed to stop the unwanted interest in her belongings that the eggs had promoted, she had sent them to me for safekeeping and to see if I could enlighten her as to what exactly they were.

\* \* \*

Dear Sir Richard,

Please accept my apologies for this unsolicited approach, but it is in desperation that I write and I don't think that there is anyone better able to help me than you. My name is Melrose, and like you I am an explorer. As I'm sure you will understand, I have come across many strange things on my travels, but I have never been so flummoxed as I have by these small dragons' eggs; four of which I enclose for your attention.

When I discovered them at an archeological dig I was immediately taken by their diminutive size and their iridescent beauty. I was permitted to remove them from the site and was taking them home for a more thorough investigation when peculiar things started to happen. Although the eggs themselves are turned to stone, or petrified, and appear completely inert, what I can only describe as "little beasts" started to creep around our belongings wherever we set up camp. At first they were easy to frighten off, but before long they became a real nuisance and gained in their temerity until they were causing quite a hindrance to our party and regularly damaging our equipment. Eventually, I could put up with the disruption no more and decided to send them to you. I have disguised them to look like pieces of jewelry in the hope that they will get to you without delay. I would greatly appreciate your thoughts and comments.

Yours most truly,

Melrose

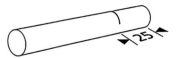

**STEP 1.** Use 1/4- to 1/2-inch dowels and mark about 25mm lengths for each mini dragon's egg you want to make.

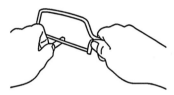

**STEP 2.** Use a hacksaw to saw the dowel to length (hold the longer end); this is good sawing practice for kids, as it is easy and safe to use a hacksaw.

**STEP 3.** Sandpaper the corners off to make the ends rounded like an egg.

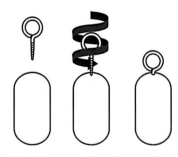

**STEP 4.** Screw a small metal eye into the center of one end. It might help to make a small hole to start with, using a nail.

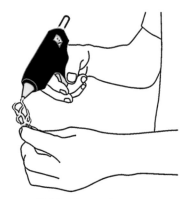

**STEP 5.** Holding the metal eye, apply a thin trickle of glue-gun glue in an organic pattern over the surface of the egg.

**STEP 6.** Put sticky tape either side of the metal eye as a mask and a handle and paint the egg in your chosen color in waterproof paint.

**STEP 7.** To distress, paint on a layer of darker acrylic thinned with water.

* * *

An hour or two in the library revealed that they were not only extremely rare examples of petrified wisp dragon eggs, but some of the finest examples of them as well. I had heard, many years before, something about miniature dragon eggs attracting the attention of the mischievous dragon imps, which can be more than a little bothersome, as they swarm over one's property in their attempts to find and recover the eggs. However, further research established that it was possible to block the effect and therefore avoid attracting the impish pests by storing the eggs in a lead-lined box, which may or may not have a one-inch sapphire window bolted to its top so that the eggs may be viewed. While I had the workshop make the required piece of equipment, I had them locked safely in the vault.

Of course, it goes without saying that I wrote back to Melrose by return, offering to keep the eggs out of harm's way until she needed them.

* * *

# The Trouble with Dragon Imps

*My Dear Melrose,*

*Thank you so much for your letter and wonderful enclosures, which I was thrilled to receive. I have never seen such fine examples of petrified wisp dragon eggs. However, I am not surprised in the least to read of your experiences with the "little beasts," as you call them, while the eggs were in your possession. Their miniature size is so enchanting and there are countless stories of travelers who, discovering such eggs, thought they had found a real treasure trove, only to have them taken back by little creatures, unknown, often resulting in the damage of personal effects or on rare occasions the loss of life.*

*The little beasts that you mention are in fact dragon imps. They are attracted by some strange property of the petrified wisp dragon eggs, I believe perhaps to be some form of radio wave emanations, although I have not been able to detect any radiation whatsoever coming from the eggs with any of the equipment we have here in our workshop at Barons Manor. It seems that the dragon imps will go to almost any lengths to recover petrified wisp eggs. Apparently, in dragon imp society, the tiny calcified eggs are highly prized. About one hundred years ago it was discovered that the only way to keep the eggs and yet avoid their detection was to hold them securely in a lead-lined box. It is not known by what mechanism the lead shields them, but it is believed that this heavy*

# Dragon Egg Pendant

**STEP 8.** Before the paint dries, wipe off with a cloth, leaving some paint in the cracks.

**STEP 9.** When dry, carefully paint silver or gold paint on the glue-gun glue lines.

**STEP 10.** Thread onto a necklace chain, gold thread, or yarn to make an attractive necklace.

*metal masks the eggs' emanations in some way. While researching the phenomenon I uncovered an old photograph of exactly such a box (which I enclose for your interest), and I have already asked my workshop to create a copy of the same so that I may store your wisp dragon eggs safely until your return, or until you send for them.*

*In the meantime, if you require replicas of the eggs, purely for display purposes, I have had some simple plans drawn up that will enable you to make extremely realistic copies, which even an expert would have trouble telling apart from the originals. In fact I must say that they make charming pendants that never fail to elicit a comment or two from admirers every time they are worn.*

*The instructions, which I trust are to your satisfaction, are attached here for your reference.*

*Your most humble servant,*

*Sir Richard*

\* \* \*

To this day Melrose has never come to collect the petrified wisp eggs, which I would very much like to put and display in our own small museum of curiosities. To this end just recently I started a project to investigate the possibility of using an alternative transparent material to house the eggs instead of the traditional sapphire (which is impossibly expensive) and yet that would still mask their broadcast. We have had some luck with quartz, but it is too early to know for sure if the crystalline substance suppresses the eggs' signal and therefore will protect us from being invaded by dragon imps when the eggs finally go on show.

The lead-lined box that protects the eggs also supports them via a low-strength "cushion field" that prevents them from touching the sides of the box. They are kept under lock and key when not being viewed. Viewing is by appointment only.

# Dragonmail Stamps

## And a story of postal delay

My father's old brother
Is quite a jet-setter,
Wherever he travels
He sends me a letter.
I'm always excited
When I get my post
Though not a big writer
He sends me the most
Incredible stamps, an
Exquisite selection,
All perfectly franked for
My stamp-book collection.

# A Story of Postal Delay

Some have neat pictures
Of kings' and queens' faces,
Or monochrome etchings
Of faraway places.
Like miniature snapshots
Of palm trees and boats,
Snow-covered mountains
Or castles with moats.

Still others show trains
With bright painted wagons,
But I love the dark ones
Of fire-breathing dragons.
It's these I collect
And arrange on my pages,
A history of monsters
Down through the ages.

This week he's flown off
To China's Guangzhou,
And promised to send me
A letter and though
This morning I waited—
It felt like too long,
Then I started thinking
That things had gone wrong.

The post usually arrives
At a quarter to eight,
So at ten minutes to
I ran down to the gate,
To see if I could see
Any sign of the postman,
His bike, or his bag,
His cat, or his post van.

But I could see no one
Nothing was there.
I trudged back to the house
And sat on the chair
In the hall by the door,
I waited, and then
After another five minutes
I went back out again.

All things being equal
You'd think that at best,
Mail stamped up correctly
And neatly addressed,
Would arrive in one's hands
Within one or two days.
So what's up with my letter?
What's caused its delays?

# Dragonmail Stamps

There's a boy in our street
With the same name as me,
He lives two doors down
At house number three.
A postal misreading?
It's an easy faux pas,
But you'd think that by now
They would know who we are.

Perhaps it went farther
And right now it's stuck
On the passenger seat
Of a post office truck,
Somewhere southwest
Of the Orbital Road,
Ten miles from my hand
At the wrong postal code.

Then ten minutes later
The housekeeper came by,
She tutted and said,
"I don't want to pry,
But shouldn't you be playing
Outside in the sun,
Not stuck here inside
On your own looking glum?"

I frowned as I answered,
"There's a very good chance
That my letter's still waiting
In Paris, in France;
Or possibly worse, and
More frustrating for me,
Becalmed on a boat
In the South China Sea."

She looked sideways at me
In the strange sort of way
That some grown-ups do when
They have something to say
But think better of it,
She sighed deeply instead,
"I don't think that boy's
Quite right in the head."

Who cares—I'd thought up
An addressing machine
That would surely reduce
Routing errors—I mean
Perhaps as I sat
It was racing the press
Across America's midwest
On the Pony Express.

# A Story of Postal Delay

Or quite possibly faster
And farther off course
Ejected from earth
With incredible force
And *NOW* in hard vacuum,
Slingshotting 'round Mars
In a royal mail rocket
On its way to the stars.

By quarter past eight
I was terribly bored
And was about to give up
When my faith was restored
By a soft sort of sound
Sounding ever so like
The voice of the postman
And the ring of his bike.

I opened the door and
Without further ado
I was handed my letter,
And immediately knew
That the stamps were all perfect;
The most beautiful kind,
All different values,
All neatly aligned.

Inside the letter
My uncle directed
"In future the house staff
Should not be subjected
To your postal neurosis!"
It was all that he wrote,
But tucked inside that
Was a ten-shilling note!

Moral of the story is that patience is a virtue seldom practiced by children.

*(You don't have to wait for your special letter to arrive. Just go to www.dragonolia. com and download these gorgeous stamps for play and your own private collection.)*

# Dragon's Egg

## And the last piece of a hundred-year-old jigsaw

The setting sun still had some warmth in it as I walked from the airport to the jetty and hailed the last water taxi to San Marco. A gentle breeze blew in off the lagoon, and pink sky, streaked with yellow clouds, bathed the quay in a warm rosy glow as I climbed gingerly into the boat.

\* \* \*

A long time ago I had the singular piece of good fortune to be given a partially reconstructed dragon's egg. Whole dragon's eggs are unheard of on account of the fact that dragon chicks usually eat the shell just after they hatch, in order to line their delicate fire bladders with flameproof minerals before their first heating. Very occasionally a dragon chick hatches, and for some reason or other doesn't eat the eggshell. When this happens, the nest may be approached, and with the dragon's permission, the broken pieces of shell collected so that the egg can be reassembled and studied. However, the egg cannot be taken from the dragon forever. Instead, as soon as it is restored, it must be presented back to the dragon within 365 days and is usually considered to be a peace offering, known to bring enormous luck to the person who returns it. Conversely, failure to return the completed egg curses those who keep it, and as a result, every dragon egg in every collection has at least one piece missing.

However broken-up the eggshell is, assembling it is not as difficult as you might think. The broken pieces have a strange magical affinity for each other, and when held close to one another, they seem to know how they fit together and direct the repairer's touch. Often, the pieces of eggshell may be separated by thousands of miles, especially if odd bits of shell have been taken from the nest at different times. Nevertheless, even the tiniest fragment of shell exerts a gentle pull on the rest of the egg at any distance, such that a sensitive person can detect the force and use it to discover the location of the missing piece or pieces.

**STEP 1.** Gently wash the egg in cold soapy water and then rinse and dry.

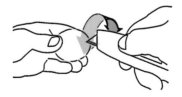

**STEP 2.** Carefully using the tip of a sharp craft knife, rotate back and forth on the same spot until you make a small hole at one end.

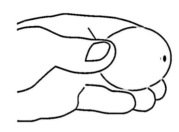

**STEP 3.** It can take up to five minutes to make a neat hole. Don't rush or force the blade, because if you do, you will crack the egg. If a bit does break away, don't worry; you can always cover it with glue later. Do the same at both ends.

**STEP 4.** Gently hold the egg to your lips and blow the contents out. Rinse the inside of the egg under a faucet and by blowing water through it.

**STEP 5.** Put some hot-melt glue on the end of a cocktail stick and glue the stick into the egg at one end. Hold steady till it is set.

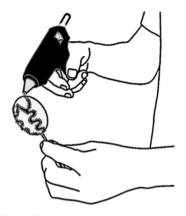

**STEP 6.** Use the glue gun to make markings on the egg's surface. Try the pattern shown, or make up any pattern you like.

i) Make loops round the top.

ii) Join them to the top of the egg with straight lines.

iii) Join them to the bottom of the egg with wavy lines.

The egg I was given had a number of pieces missing, and over the hundred years or so that it has been in my possession, whenever the opportunity has presented itself, I have sought out the errant parts and slowly but surely reassembled the egg. Now with only one piece left, I could barely contain my excitement as the taxi sped over the mirror-calm sea toward Venice and the resting place of the last piece.

The glittering lights of San Marco's cafés and restaurants played on the water, as I paid the taxi and climbed up to the cobbled square.

In my breast pocket, the subtle tug of the egg grew stronger and stronger as I walked across the piazza. I relaxed and cleared my thoughts so that I might better feel its pull and allow it to take me in the right direction. I had already determined the approximate location of the last piece by using an ancient map and a remote divining skill I had learned in Tibet, but it was not until I was standing outside the tiny mask shop in Calle D'Angelo that I knew for certain that I had found the last piece of shell. I took a deep breath and pushed the door. It swung open easily, jangling a small bell that hung above it and flooding my senses with the dazzling colors of a thousand handmade masks. Every single inch of the walls and ceiling was crammed to bursting with layer upon layer of brilliantly painted faces, nearly every one gilded to some degree in either silver or gold. Some were trimmed with exotic feathers, while others sparkled with diamanté and glass rubies. But even those that were just painted shone in such a rich, vibrant saturation that it was impossible to think that whole new palettes hadn't been invented in their creation.

I glanced around the shop, hardly daring to breathe, and one mask immediately caught my eye. I was about to call out to the proprietor when I was startled by a voice from the back of the shop.

"I am sorry, signore."

I looked around to see the shop-keeper, who nodded up at the mask I had been staring at.

"The dragon mask, signore. I'm sorry, it's not for sale."

I thought for a second and was about to take out the egg and explain

**STEP 7.** Paint or spray the egg with a permanent paint.

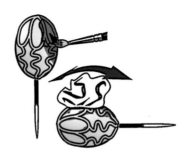

**STEP 8.** To distress, paint black acrylic paint over the egg. While painting wipe paint off with a damp cloth, so that the black paint stays in all the cracks and dips, so that the egg looks old.

**STEP 9.** Touch up with gold paint or any other colors you want. When the egg is dry, cut off the cocktail stick with wire cutters or strong scissors.

**STEP 10.** Trace around the template and transfer the shape onto a medium-weight card or thick, stiff paper if you have it. Carefully cut out using a craft knife or strong scissors.

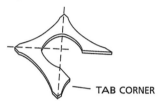

TAB CORNER

**STEP 11.** Turn over the cutout and deep crease from corner to corner on the back on the three corners that have folds. That is, the two main corners and the tab corner.

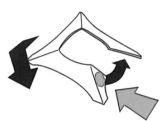

**STEP 12.** Turn back over and fold the stand at the creases. Put a blob of hot glue, or white glue (white glue will take a while to dry and will need to be held while drying), or a small piece of double-sided sticky tape onto the tab and glue the tab neatly to the inside of the free corner.

**STEP 13.** Color, paint, or spray the finished stand. Now your stand is ready to present your dragon's egg.

myself when I noticed that it was starting to get hot in my pocket, and that wasn't all. The shopkeeper himself was looking very strange. He was shaking slightly and was turning redder and redder by the second. The air crackled with static and I felt the hairs on my arms prickling. The keeper staggered slightly and I had to put my arm out to steady him.

"I cannot sell it to you," he said falteringly, looking at me with widening eyes, "but you may take it . . . yes, take it, signore, as a gift," he said finally, in a rush.

I didn't wait for him to change his mind, or for the power of the egg to diminish. With some difficulty he wrapped the mask and I left the shop as quickly as I could. As soon as I reached the safety of my hotel room, I unwrapped the mask and searched it for the tiny fleck of golden shell that had remained hidden within its decoration for what must have been decades. It wasn't hard to find, disguised in plain view as a single golden teardrop under the dragon's right eye. With shaking hands, I gently lifted it free using tweezers and fitted it into place in the dragon's egg.

# The Final Piece of the Jigsaw

I hardly noticed the journey back, distracted as I was with thoughts of how the egg should be returned. Now that I'm back at Barons Manor, I am writing to you to see if you have any ideas as to whom I should give the egg, so that they might present it back to the dragon and gain everlasting good fortune. I have had more than my fair share of luck over the years and I am not in need of any more. So it is with this last note that, Dear Reader, I humbly ask your advice. I have prepared a place at www.dragonolia.com especially for you to leave your suggestions—but hurry, for as you already know, the egg must be returned within 365 days.

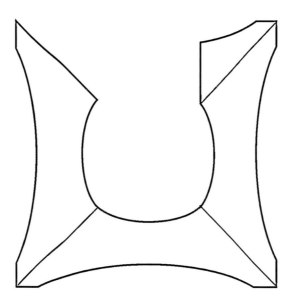

***Dragon's egg stand template***